THE WORLD
I USED TO KNOW

The Best of
WALTER RINDER

PHOTOS &
TEXT BY WALTER RINDER

Celestial Arts
Berkeley, California

This material revised by the author and selected from *Love Is an Attitude*, *This Time Called Life*, *The Humanness of You*, *Love is My Reason*, and *Will You Share With Me?*.

CELESTIAL ARTS
P.O. Box 7327
Berkeley, California 94707

Cover design by Ken Scott
Cover photo by Walter Rinder
Text photos by Walter Rinder
Composition by Ann Flanagan Typography
Set in Berkeley Old Style

Library of Congress Card Catalog Number:
89-81211

ISBN 0-89087-596-0

First Printing, 1990

Manufactured in the United States of America

T*he World I Used To Know* is the best of my writings, gathered from five of my books published in the seventies but also influenced by the decade of the sixties.

Those of you who have my books will find familiar writings that have touched your hearts. Those of you who will discover me for the first time, I hope will feel a contribution to your lives as you read these pages.

This little book is made to carry with you as a companion edition in your everyday living. It is a source of inspiration in guiding your hopes and dreams through the congestion and conflicts of our de-humanizing society.

Whether in your purse or in your back pocket, this book is a lifelong friend who cares about you.

Share it with others that they may know of your humanness. It speaks of a gentle spirit, a romantic nature, and a sharing that wishes to find acceptance.

We arrive in this world alone, we depart alone, this time called life was meant to share.

Walter Rinder

To those precious moments of life,
I dedicate this book, for giving me
the experiences, courage, and
ability to touch your life ... then!

                    now!

LOVE
IS
AN
ATTITUDE

I had a special place when I clawed
my way to freedom, away from the city
        Meditating upon the rocks
        melting into the icy water
        inhaling the salt air—
my mind commenced to heal
I wrote...I thought...I swam...
I slept...I watched
One day a stranger entered my domain
and my solitude was transformed
into love

Nothing is more wondrous than a
    human being
when he begins to discover himself.

Music echoed across…valleys and mountains and cities where he called home, even for but a short while. The songs he sang were as the **minstrels**, folk songs and short episodes of his wonderings.

We used to listen to his tales in front of the old red house, when he once came our way, and we drifted into his world with him. We never knew where he came from or where he was going. He made our lives a little fuller and set us to thinking.

Yesterday's hurt
  Is today's understanding
    Rewoven into tomorrow's love.

Don't look away from the world
Give yourself to it.

Because you are afraid to love
I am alone.

The tide washes in...
I walk with thoughts of the dreamer's wine
and a thousand nights pass
mirrored by the sea.

Which has more substance, the
thought of love or
an act of love?

Will we see the day when,
again, nature becomes the
teacher of man?

The soul can rise from the earth
into the sky, like a bird
aware of its freedom,
not feeling the barriers of man
but the beauty of love
which is eternal.

To My Beloved

I love you freely without restrictions
I love your understanding without doubt
I love you honestly without deceit
I love you creatively without conditioning
I love you now without reservation
I love you physically without pretending
I love your soul without wishing
I love your being without wanting
I love you.

All that we love deeply
becomes a part of us.

We are all mirrors unto one another.
Look into me and you will find something
of yourself as I will of you.

Day has vanished. The sun has dropped like a penny into the pocket of the night. The sounds of the daylight hours have given way to quiet solitude. Fog is creeping in, engulfing the cypress trees, erasing my view of the ocean, hiding the moon that lights my wandering along the shore.

Where are you! Where did you go! Let me feel your touch. Don't let this moment slip away from us. Listen, hear, the sea gull. He's searching, too. Please take my hand; it's extended for you.

See the footprints in the sand, traveling from shore to shore. The tide will wash away those footprints, but tomorrow there will be new ones. There always are. Take my hand. We've a long way to go. A lifetime.

I was alone, walking in the park.
You were sitting by a tree.
Our eyes met.
You smiled.
I returned the smile.
In that moment we knew.

I fear no love—
For my heart is open,
My mind sincere,
And my actions honorable.

Do not reject what you do not
understand; for with understanding
there may be acceptance.

Hands

Our hands are extensions of our heart, through their movements people know what we are, who we are, and how we feel.

Take hold of someone's hand. You can feel the beating of their heart, the very substance of their life.

The hand has as many expressions as the face, and if you don't see any reactions from the face, watch their hands . . . covering their face in desperation, reaching out for warmth, caressing your body with love, clawing to push death away, tension in holding something, their motion in creating, their movements in happiness, stillness in idleness or loneliness.

The shape of the hands follows the structure of the body, heavy, thin, muscular, fragile, strong, smooth, rough.

Our mind is the energy, our hands the projection of that energy.

Take someone's hand and you will have, in that moment, begun the awareness of yourself. That moment has the seed of the creation of love, every time it is done.

Use your hands in the pursuit of beauty, adding and building of life.

The hands are so very sensitive to the elements of nature. Feel the bark of a tree. Put your hands in the snow of a cold stream. Run your fingers across the sand. Put your hands near a fire. Hold your hands up to the rain or the sun or the wind, all different feelings. Touch the coat of a dog or the skin of a snake.

As the years pass, your hands gain knowledge as does your mind, and grow older as does your body.

Your hands carry episodes of your life: scarred, stained, calloused, scratched.

Let your hands become the joining together of you and another human being, the extension of your heart, the merging of two rivers, the grafting of two branches, the birth of new life.

Your hands are you.

Last night it rained. I saw your face through the clouded window pane. It seemed you were crying, but it was only the rain falling down the window. I heard your laughter, but it was only the thunder repeating itself. I thought I heard you talking to me, but it was only the branches rubbing against the glass.

It's morning now. The rain has stopped.

The harmony and balance
of nature is one of
the greatest lessons to man.

Have you ever listened to the snowfall?

To be of few words and to be of many actions is to follow the path of nature.

A storm does not drop all its rain in one place, nor does a river have one tributary, or is there just one wave in the ocean, or does the sun always shine. Rather, a continued variation and repetition of acts gives the harmony and balance to nature. This is what we should strive for: Love in all forms and all kinds becomes the harmony of man.

Help me to unite myself with life
through your love.

We *should receive love*
with as much understanding
as we give love.

Remember by finding things
within yourself
only then will you be able to
share them with others.

On this "Speck of Earth," together we can make love, only if we transform ourselves into the trees and vegetation that surround us, so that we are not seen by human beings. For someone, somewhere will say of us, "our love is wrong."

They don't understand!

Remember

When you ran along the rocky caves
discovered the oceans white capped waves
when you dreamed of crystal clear lagoons
making love, in youth, by the light of
        the moon
when you saw the sun in all its splendor
touched a rose so soft and tender
felt the rain against your cheek
saw a fawn so shy and meek
when you played in the snow of yesterday
or slept in the barn on a mound of hay
when you planted your garden in early
        spring

or sat by a campfire while everyone sings
remember the touch of a hand or the smile
     on a face
or the home that was blessed by your
     parents' grace
the little green tree so happy and bright
that was dressed all in colors on that
     christmas night
or the sounds of the birds or the stars in
     the sky
or your home-made kite you used to fly
remember, remember these things that
     you've done
  and think of your youth when you're
     teaching your son.

People of Earth

How accelerated your lives have become ... not begun! ... you ... people of the earth, integrated into ant hills you call cities. Caught in the whirlpool of your society, bringing you deeper and deeper into your jungle of asphalt, cement mountains covering the sun, stagnant air as your sky, status symbols of synthetics, overcrowding, waiting in lines, hurrying to where! Freeways, byways, traffic jams, headaches, tension, alcohol, drugs, insecurity, not caring, being afraid ... and whatever happened to love?

You surround yourselves with progress, like living on an island without a boat.

Are you really happy? Does progress bring a fulfillment within your soul?

You are a part of nature, you come from the earth, from the seed of life. You are alienated when you depart from the original beauty of your environment. You possess a soul. So does nature ... And when you are together, you speak deep thoughts, not in words, but in feelings ...

REMEMBER ... when the warm sun followed you as you ran freely along the ocean's shores; the sand was warm when your feet pressed into its softness; the wind was pure as it lifted your hair dancing to the rhythm of your movements; and how the salt water tingled your body as it dried crisp on your golden skin ... THE SUN WAS ALIVE.

REMEMBER ... when you heard the laughter of the waves as they splashed and played with the rocks; the harmonious colors of the ocean as she dressed for the new day; and the gentle kiss of the water as it died in the arms of the shore to be reborn again far out at sea … THE OCEAN WAS ALIVE.

REMEMBER … the little tide pool you found hidden among the rocks; so serene, so clean, so transparent, and within its depths lay pieces of colored shells, a starfish or two; beautiful emerald green sea urchins; delicate pink anemones; and tiny fish darting to and fro; a world within a world … THE POOL WAS ALIVE.

As you began departing from nature, nature said of you: "I know man is leaving me, but I welcome him to return when he wishes, for I love him and want him to always be a part of me, sharing our hidden secrets." You seldom went back to nature and all is almost forgotten … PROGRESS HAS ENSLAVED YOU … PROGRESS HAS BECOME A TYRANT AND YOU HIS SLAVE … FREE YOURSELVES … people of earth.

Cut the shackles that bind you. Open the door of your mind, TO AWARENESS—as you look into the sky, into the ocean, upon the valleys and the mountains, and you will shed tears of happiness as you feel the rain run down your cheeks, as you feel the snow-flakes melt in your hands, as you feel the sun give warmth to your body, as you feel the wind embrace you.

FOR IN NATURE WITH
MAN THERE IS LOVE ...
SHARING ...
   FAITHFUL ...
   ETERNAL.

When you have freed yourself from the dogma and conditioning of your society, where will you go? To those things you love.

Let your mind and your actions explode with awareness as you light your forgotten lanterns of happiness, as you find a peaceful clearing in the jungle of your society.

Love is everywhere. It is in the night sky where the stars smile. It is the field of wheat dancing in the wind. It is the waves sculpturing the rocks. It is in the sound of music, in man's creation of art. It is a seed nourished by two human beings.

Love will find you.

You will find love, if . . .

LOVE BECOMES
YOUR ATTITUDE

A thousand years is but a
grain of sand in time...but love
is a thousand grains of sand in
one human lifetime.

THIS TIME CALLED LIFE

What we call life

We arrive in this world alone ... this time called life was meant to share.

Under the cover of the stars,
under the cover of the sun fermented into
   eternity
there lies a precious moment of time we call
   life.
A gift of Creation.
We are given minds to discover,
talent to create,
curiosity to gain knowledge,
insight to build,
emotions to communicate our feelings,
and movement through our physical body.

Open your gift!

Sometimes I feel like a bird

Sometimes I feel like a
  bird
free in its flight,
but constantly aware
of looking for a place to rest;
searching for food to fill
the hunger within. And in my
freedom of movement, like the
  bird,
we both are creatures of needs.
      They must be fulfilled.

Close to earth

Close to the earth
where the wind blows free
a man sets down roots
for his children to see

They learn from the deer
Its swiftness in flight
They learn from the bear
Its strength and its might

They learn from the bird
Its grace and its songs
They learn from the snake
Where they don't belong

They learn from the flowers
Their colors and smells
They learn from the waters
To seek their own wells

As the seasons pass by
a man in his toil
knows that his children
Have learned from the soil

Their hearts filled with love
Their spirit unchained
His children aren't sculptured
with fear or with pain

Close to the earth
where the wind blows free
a man sets down roots
for his children to see

Aura of life

Winter's aura
brings the snow
also makes the fires glow

Spring's young aura
brings new birth
also shows a man his worth

Summer's aura
brings the sun
sends its children on the run

Autumn's aura
brings the wind
that makes the leaves to gaily spin

Through all the seasons
we learn the reasons

I saw life through the eyes of a child
as I watched him clean his boat
before putting it into the lake.
   We can learn from children.

Wherever we are together—
that be our home—
for a home is where people love

Remember the good times

at the sea

when we tore our shells away, our emotions
poured forth—lying in the sand, your head
resting on my chest, you listening to the
impatient beating of my heart—or me to
yours.

with the sky

when we ran down the hills to the rhythm
of the clouds, laughing at the rain, kissing
your wet lips, crying because of our
overabundance of happiness.

in the mountains

beneath the waterfall where we made our
commitment, to stay together forever
I truly believe we meant it then

Life constantly changes reality

Did we dwell too long under the spell of
    love's dreams?
Were we hypnotized not to move with the
    essence of life?
Did our love drift apart by the turbulence
    of the
        winds of change?

   goodbye

remember the good times

He had one arm ... one leg
nineteen, I think
he smiled at me
I returned the smile
he smiled at someone else
they turned away

Now that we have touched

Now that we have touched, where do
   we go
from here? Why must actions be only
   moments?
The stagnant pond omits life.
You know non-movement can do that,
just sitting still!

His love was ... simple, uninhibited
    child like, spontaneous
    filled with touching, giving roses
        poetry

he never grew up ...
        thank goodness!

———————

Is it my silence you fear the most or
my actions? If I move freely within
myself, you draw away and begin to run.
        Come back!

———————

I met a human being; we shared many
    hours together.
He said as he left that evening, "I'll see you
around sometime." He never even knew
    my name!

Fullness of love

If there were two loves ...
    I would choose them both

The bridge

My friend,
I have built a bridge for you
to cross over to me ...
but not a vehicle
    to carry you

Returning

He runs
    to meet the setting of the sun
        following roads
            to nowhere
            somewhere
            he doesn't care
    keep going lad, become free
        no going back
        back to what?
    explore
        experience
            develop
                change
run
    to meet the setting of the sun

A friend is
   someone with whom you can probe his
      soul without fear . . .
   of your acceptance
            seeking his knowledge

A friend is
   someone with whom you can lie next to
      and hold without fear . . .
   of his attitude toward your intentions
            seeking his warmth

A friend is
   someone with whom you can plan time
      to share
         without fear . . .
   of his indifference
            seeking his honor

A friend is
   in truth a human being
      there is no fear . . .
   your life, which is precious, is shared
            seeking your peace

Understanding

Raindrops never care to stay
nor clouds on passing by
or will rainbows let you touch them
as they arch upon the sky

A waterfall is never still
nor leaves in autumn season
or wind that bends the marsh grass down
that gives no apparent reason

Our footsteps trod on many paths
beneath the cover of the sky
for man has shown by living
we find the reasons, why

Travel far, my weary friend
with nature's careful planning
touch the flowers of the soul
then wait, for understanding

"I'm a boy you see"

I once knew a man
Who felt love for me
But I couldn't return it
For I'm a boy, you see.

Our society has taught me
What is right, what is wrong
I'm conditioned I feel
But I know not how long.

> Will I die a boy to be a man
> Will my soul fly free, or sink in the sand

The sound of his words
The feel of his touch
It is fear that I feel
Though I love him so much.

Why when we lay
So close in the night
The division between us
Brings together our plight.

     Will I die a boy to be a man
     Will my soul fly free, or sink in the sand

"I love you", he'd say
"No shame do I hold
For my feelings are natural
It's the world that is cold."

His thoughts were like spears
Cast deep in my heart
For the world it has taught me
I should have no part

Of his touch or affection
Of his wanting to give

I'm being pulled apart
By this life that I live

    Will I die a boy to be a man
    Will my soul fly free, or sink in the sand

Love is the answer
I know, oh I know!
But How do I show Him
When fear rules me so

I toss and I turn
I stumble, I fall
I spin like a top
Till it hits the wall

My brain, it's exploding
My feelings need air
It's an unnatural life
When people don't care

Will I die a boy to be a man
Will my soul fly free, or sink in the sand

When will I open
My love for this man
Being proud and happy
To take hold of his hand

I once knew a man
Who felt love for me
But I couldn't return it
For I'm a boy, you see

Will I die a boy to be a man
Will my soul fly free, or sink in the sand?

We Fled

From the city we fled
to snow covered mountains
The sun followed our day
exploring a magnificent world that
we might have known
but not together
sharing worlds we did know
together ...
a small waterfall
by the road
icicles ... sculptured
pine branches
snow in their hands
waving to us
when the wind arose
clouds by the multitudes

in wondrous patterns
as if creation were painting
a canvas for us ...
trees of pure gold
standing like sentinels
by the brooding hills
ashamed of their nakedness
in and among this we spoke
our words floated to the earth
with the snowflakes
covering the ground
the love shadows came
with night's approach
as we sat on the fence
watching the canvas completed
the painting was for us ...

Round

Man   woman
man   man
woman   woman
all on the ferris wheel of life
paired lovers   united
married couples   divided
all on the ferris wheel of life

around and around goes the wheel
faster and faster this circle of steel
concrete and asphalt go whizzing by
come ride with me as we pierce the sky
man and boy   daring
girl and woman   sharing
hippy and straight   comparing
establishment   staring
all on the ferris wheel of life

our government in   contemplation
our society in   condemnation
our police in   retaliation
our youth in   meditation ...
rebuilding a new foundation
all on the ferris wheel of life

around and around goes the wheel
faster and faster this circle of steel
concrete and asphalt go whizzing by
come ride with me as we pierce the sky

    I'm getting dizzy
      let me off!

I cry

I cry when I see indifference
as a man lies in the street
people walk on by his hurts
with scared and frightened feet

I cry when on the radio
I hear the dying of young men
who traveled to some foreign land
never to see their home again

I cry when I see a young girl
engulfed in unnatural highs
as she escapes reality
trying to find the reasons why!

I cry when I feel the heartbeat
of a lonely soul's embrace
for I know what they are feeling
I've been to that same place

I cry for earth's humanity
for its destiny may become
a void and empty planet
moving listlessly around the sun

I cry because I have the faith
so deep within my heart
that man can change the ugliness
that has always been a part

Of human movement in all times
the values have been placed
on superficial attitudes
a stigma of the human race.

Being

Climb to the threshold of
your own beliefs,
not with the statement
of others,
but with the footsteps of
your own experience

Know yourself . . .

Experience life
by crawling in its dirt and
being lifted by the wings of its beauty.

Christmas Eve

Here in the country, everyone has gone to friends' or relatives' homes for their traditional Christmas, and I am left alone. But in spirit I have been given a splendor beyond man's deepest dreams, for before my eyes is a wonderland so magnificent, so inspiring that if there were angels they would be crying tears of joy.

I am surrounded by a whole forest of the most beautiful, pine scented, living Christmas trees, reaching toward the sky a hundred times taller than myself. At the tips of these trees are thousands of stars shining and twinkling and sparkling everywhere I look. All around me is an aura of Christmas music; the little stream I am sitting by is a choir of many voices singing the carols of Christmas, my two dogs running back and forth across the old wooden bridge are the sound of the cymbals and drums, every so often a night bird cries out like Christmas chimes, the wind blowing through the branches are the violins playing Silent Night, the frogs are the horns and the crickets the flutes, and together they all are my symphony of Christmas, present.

My Christmas is a living, real experience. Even Tom-Tom our turkey looks far more beautiful in his pen, his autumn colored feathers fanned out with such pride, than cooked sitting on the table.

Thank you for your Christmas gifts to me and for the mistletoe high in the trees, the pine cones sitting on the branches, the red berries on the bushes, the acorns on the ground and the poinsettias growing near the barn. You have given unto me the dis-covery on this Christmas Eve that the most valued of gifts we can give or receive is the meaning of life through personal experience.

New Journey

When tomorrow becomes today, start packing for your new journey. Put your old attitudes to which you no longer relate in the trunk along with those material possessions for which you will no longer have a need. In the suitcase of your mind, leave plenty of room for love. On your journey you will be collecting many new feelings as your soul and dignity expand into a high consciousness.

Oh lonely boy

As I walked along the country road
on a peaceful winter's day
I came upon a boy alone
which fate had brought my way

With sleeping bag upon his back
an unshaven, love-worn face
he showed a friendly, youthful smile
a smile of human grace

I said to him, "Good morning lad
What is your given name
Where is it that you come from
mountains, city or distant plain?"

In tired words of certainty
he said as he sat down
"My search is long and endless
as I travel town to town

I've wandered here, I've wandered there
exploring far and wide
longing to breathe the breath of love
holding its life inside

I've been on city streets
in early morning hours
I've walked the country roads
smelling fragrant, petaled flowers

I've awakened in motel rooms
in the middle of the night
thinking all I had for company
was the conscience of my plight

I've sat upon the pilings
of a wharf where ocean flows
visioned countless human faces
in my memory of long ago

I've been in movie houses
watching lives in love and pain
my head bending on my shoulders
as the tears would fall like rain

I've met a stranger on the street
we shared the cloud filled day
but when the night bounced back again
we went our separate ways

So now you've heard my story
thank you for your time
there are many miles to cover
before nightfall rests my mind."

He arose and stood before me
reaching out to hold my hand
the last words he softly spoke
echoed loud, across our land

"Will I die a starved, unwanted boy
from the love I never find
or live my years in searching
leaving bits of me behind

Or will I find the love I need
sharing each and every day
in the beauty of togetherness
and my journey ends that way?"

Song

Turquoise made mountains
tangerine skies
apple gold meadows
where the wizard abides

Emerald deep plains
bronze orchards shown bright
pastel colored rainbows
which give us our light

Bushes sweet laughter
trees that can walk
children that sing with
the flowers that talk

Indigo wheat fields
burnt sienna stars
a sun wrapped in silver
that seeds wisdom afar

The green pebbled path
through forests red cloak
down canyons of purple

to this wizard of oak

Clouds bushing our cheeks
waves gentle hands
thunder soft and mellow
raining amber sand

Where peace is abundant
a world—love inborn
the wizard of lovers
exiles man's bestial scorn

Where embracing is natural
kisses live free
affection glows fire
and we can just be

Journey my beloved
to my harmony land
where the wizard eternal
holds sceptre in hand

All are paired lovers
with nothing to fear
for love is the purpose
in the voices we hear.

Fragments

Too many people are only fragments of
   themselves
        for others to see

become a whole human being

Awareness

On a day when a man condemns me for
what I say and for my actions
may I also be sent the courage,
through my knowledge of love,
to stand before his wrath;
not in the quicksand of submission,
but on the solid rock of my own
awareness.

Beyond this path

Beyond the curved path
across the stone arched bridge
above the etched cliff
towering high over trees
beneath the shroud of fog
… it began its descent
into space
cascading
free from barriers
      we stared in wonderment
no words to speak
we were learning
from its touch
there were no barriers

Precious moments

Don't exclude yourself ... from
    precious moments
warm encounters
        beautiful attitudes
      majestic discoveries
        flowing intimacies
           sensory development

for these are the jewels
placed in the crown of your destiny

Tidepools

You've shown me unknown worlds
    on the face of leaves
    under forest logs
    inside ocean tidepools
    within small pockets on cliffs
Yet the hidden world of my soul
      still remains a mystery

Naked

He walked naked along the stream
children giggled
        laughing funny faces
people whispered
        sang their silly tunes
he was a fragment of the natural

Dedicated to my Mom
and Dad

When you were criticizing me
and finding here and there
a fault or two to speak of
or a weakness you could tear

There are many human failures
in the average of us all
and many grave shortcomings
into which we do fall

When you were blaming me for meanness
or misunderstanding my words of truth
you remembered in this world of ours
life's not easy in our youth

I've struggled through many a sorrow
I've waded through many a fear
I've had the strength and courage
to laugh through many a tear

In my young years you had the patience
through your love to understand
building your son's self-confidence
to become a gentle man

Time

Between crevices, hued in stone
runs the waves in symphonic tones
toward the shore its destiny
from time of birth within the sea

Raining spray with joyful glee
surging forward momentously
rocks stand fast against their might
as waves leap up above the rocks height

Churning waters restless path
moves beside these rocks to laugh
waves enclose their sullen faces
sentinels standing in monotonous
    unchosen places

Black these giants of the shore
who in time will be no more
as boundless sea with caps of white
traveling passed in endless flight

Death awaits on yonder sand
as I watch through eyes of man
waters body twist and turn
their journey's end, I stand and learn

Life flows free

Upon the butte he stood
sunlight filtered window shown
walls of mountains, his house enclosed
in this land, his home

sagebrush moved upon his floor
pussywillows adorned his door
gnarled scrub oak his treasured art
hawks throughout his house would dart

canyoned hallways
valleyed rooms
vases filled
with desert blooms

knowledge gained
in fossiled rocks
red winged bird
perched on hollyhocks

half moon hills
spilled amber and blue
skies constant change
into evening hue

there was a void
he knew not his worth
a time when he questioned
why of his birth

city's faded memory
confusion was gone
now life flowed free
as the rivers song

We can gain knowledge without
   wisdom
We cannot gain wisdom without
   knowledge

Possess not the soul of another
   human being
for the abundance of your fruit may break
   the branch

Thinking of love is life's mirage
acting in love is life's oasis

It is not by words alone that a person is
    revealed to us
but in our perception of his silence that we
    know him best

Truth within us is silent
conditioning is the voice so often spoken

A man can become blind
if he continues to
walk in the shadow
of his soul's own
enlightenment

I give you a gift of yourself
wrapped in my love

Each man should develop the most
from the natural gifts of his body and mind
for a sense of personal achievement

Loneliness can be a lack of responding
to your environment

If we suspect the motive
we quite often condemn the act

Life is the endless beauty of unity

Our motives, whether honorable
  or fraudulent,
truly justify our actions

The stagnant pond omits life
non movement can do that
just sitting still

Look for the Good in yourself
Not the evil in others

The spirit of an action or deed is far more
important than the action, for in the
intention lies the beauty or ugliness

Love can travel a thousand miles
without a sound

We walk with our head looking down
    at the dust
instead of lifting our eyes toward the
    horizon

Truth in one man may be folly in another
yet we carry both

If a man shows you a new path in life,
    ask not
that he walk before you, ask only if he has
walked that path

Touch a human being so they may know
    you're there
for so many are blind and deaf

                Words, can keep us apart

Only one today

I truly have given
everyway I know how
in all of my actions
that you will allow

I've struggled in knowledge
in logic and thought
to tear down your barrier
this wall that I've fought

I've hidden affection
when you weren't aware
not to push you away
from me, so I bare

This hurt and involvement
of love's tender touch
and live in my prison
called "I love you so much"

I've reached out my hand
when I thought you were drowning
for I stood alone
while life stands there clowning

I've acted unwisely
at times, this I've felt
But the things that were done
were with love's flowing help

I've cried in the night
when you were so near
and my tears went unseen
because of my fear

Why can't we see
this wall that we share
for we both want to give
and we both truly care

There are many tomorrows
but only one today
The longer we wait
in finding a way

To freely express
our faith in each other
this idea man calls love
that you are my lover

Time moves us away
lives drift us apart
our needs they surrender
to the hurts of the heart

This reality can change
let's show the world
our love for each other
flows natural, unfurled

That they may gain hope
from our interacting life
and we rise from the dust
of humanity's strife

For the children unborn
we will build a foundation
if together we project
our love and elation

in the truths we have found
by opening ourselves
to the love of each other
filling our own wells

There are many tomorrows
but only one today.
The longer we wait
the harder the way.

I am

I was born of an emotion
bursting, into the world a tear
Discard your mask!
I must stream down your face
　　for I am life . . .

We arrive upon this earth
                              alone
we depart
            alone
this time called life, was meant to share.

LOVE IS
MY
REASON

The Letter

My dear friend;

The cycles of my life came and went as my wrinkles became more pronounced and the trees grew taller but fewer. Once in awhile I'd find a stray white hair in my beard, not yet stained by pollution.

Turmoil continues between countries. Peace is still not as popular as is war. New inventions keep making life easier, my people fatter, and more dependent. Science is accelerating at a fantastic pace, changing our society with its magic while more artificial stimulants are being found to replace the simple universal qualities of the individual.

Progress is my people's creed and nature feels the brunt of our new life, liberty and the pursuit of happiness. Our government is performing many miracles with welfare and food stamps and unemployment benefits which too often become substitutes for human incentive. Poverty of the mind is massacring healthy human bodies. Our rich become more influential and our poor become more abundant. Being stoned on drugs, booze or money is still the false enlightenment of many.

Our youth inherit what our social order has created. I personally feel we are seducing our young people by not giving them the freedom to be themselves, forcing them to accept our thinking without choice and scaring them into submission by threatening them with God concepts of good and evil. Interpretation of social conduct should come from love—a love so expansive that our imagination cannot fathom any boundaries.

Our Creator was so wise in giving man free choice. Each man must wade through the debris of many thoughts and concepts to find his own original innocence and truth. Nothing is absolute, so all judgments must be flexible to allow the discovery of universal truths for all men and individual truths which create difference. Our people must be able to know (not just think) that each one of us possesses a free spirit.

A government or church can only guide a person's thoughts, suggest ideas of behavior where loving is concerned. I am saddened each time I am told a person is afraid to show me love. It's not that they don't feel love or affection, it's just that somewhere in the past someone in authority taught them to separate loving into categories of right and wrong. Great pain occurs when man legislates loving.

Maybe *your* country, my friend, is a place of tranquility and untouched beauty unfolding majestic mountains, rivers and the coastal regions of *your* land. Maybe *your* cities abound with flowers and trees and acres of clover and grasses, and *your* small buildings reflect the personality of *your* people. Maybe *your* people collect feelings instead of things. Maybe *your* lives are uncomplicated and filled with the richness of love. Maybe I could share *my* life with you, in love, and live out *my* years without suffering or suppression; but I'm sorry, my friend, I cannot forsake *my* country. It has helped to make *me* what I am—what you love about *me*. I cannot run away from the boundless energy and potential that lies deep within *my* people.

We are young, have much to learn, and have made many mistakes. We have growing pains, and our greed and money hunger may someday strip us of our creature comforts, power and blind acceptance, showing us in stead humility and compassion for difference. We may one day tear down the monuments we built to our inflated egos. The ignorant men who now control our lives may topple from their thrones because we little people will care enough to get involved; to change, to dedicate our lives to the rebuilding of a society built upon all types of love as the reason.

I feel I am still in the promised land, my friend, where love is now beginning to direct our destinies. My choice to stay was made years ago, for this is my home—from the Pacific to the Atlantic—from Canada to Mexico. I was born on her soil and my flesh and bones will go back into her earth, nurturing new growth.

Should she ever fall, her society crumbling and decaying from internal strife, I (and others like me) will find the strength and determination to pick up the scattered pieces, to help rebuild and become a better example for the world.

Thank you for your love, your offers of sharing, and your concern for my happiness and well-being, but I must stay here. Here I will try to construct a better way, to leave my footprints on her history so future generations will know I once lived, bled, suffered, loved and cared enough to fight for a man's free spirit and the beauty of the individual. My people are a part of me and as they hurt so do I. As they live with injustice so do I. As long as the individual nature is repressed by social order. I cannot find personal peace—my soul is linked like a chain to my people's bondage.

How can any man divorce himself from the simple, unrestricted love of his fellow man when we all belong to the same creator, to the same family, to the same planet, to the same universe and have the same love within us all?

Must I have a reason to love you; cannot love be my reason?

LOVE IS MY REASON

WILL YOU SHARE
WITH ME?

Simple Things

I have come to know the simple things in life that help to make the complex mind silent of many frustrations.

the sound of leaves
the knocking on my door of a friend
a forest illuminated by the moon
the smell of fireplace smoke as I walk down
   the road
a frog hiding in the foliage with her family
picking huckleberries from the bushes

making rose hip tea from wild roses
finding sour grass and mushrooms for a
   salad
waking up to the sound of a river
eating homemade bread baked in my
   kitchen
building a woodshed beneath the pines
discovering new flowers
finding old things in a homestead
feeling the earth ... breathing.

The Great White Mountain

We hiked all morning up the slope of the mountain, through the cover of trees, to the top. Sitting on the top we looked over the ridges, into the valleys which separated these giant mounds of earth.

The Indians once sat on this very spot worshipping the Great Spirit, honoring the season of their hunt, for this was their hunting ground. A time when bear roamed in vast numbers eating the huckleberries and catching salmon and steelhead trout in the radiant streams and rivers that wound their way through the corridor that led to the Great White Mountain. Deer and beaver were plentiful, as were the ducks and grouse and pheasants. There was plenty for all, for life was in balance. The predator sought out his prey and the prey would many times evade the predator. As things died, new life was born upon the mountains and the balance continued. Then one day the white man entered this domain. The Great White Mountain accepted him with suspicion for the mountain had seen what the white man had done to the lands in the east.

More and more men came and as they came they began to plunder and rape, taking advantage of the hospitality that the Great White Mountain offered them in her bounty. They began to strip her naked, cutting down the trees, catching the beaver and bears for fur, shooting the deer and ducks.

Now, a hundred years later, the Great White Mountain can be seen weeping, for she has witnessed the destruction of balance in her domain. Most of her beautiful creatures are gone and a very few old trees stand to tell the tale of the white man's ax and saw.

As I sat upon this rock, my eyes scanning the countryside, I too felt the shame and sorrow of what man had done, for all the beauty of nature that I would never see, or feel, nor would my children. I looked up toward the Great White Mountain feeling a small degree of the pain she must feel, watching her children destroyed. I got up and walked over to a clump of wildflowers and bent down to kiss them and the tears fell from my eyes upon their petals and at that moment the earth began to tremble and the clouds began to swirl faster, and the wind swept down between the mountains, and I felt the Great White Mountain saying:

What has been ravished by your people can never be reclaimed, my son, but you can protect what little remains so that once again beauty shall inherit the earth.

Senses

In the woods my senses have become
extremely alert to the sounds and smells,
many strange to me.

One day while exploring near a waterfall
I found a beautiful clump of mushrooms
hiding in a dead log.

I had discovered another link in the
universal chain of life which binds us
together.

In the Shadow of the Mountain

In the shadow of the mountain
there lived a boy of a restless age
neither time nor people could hold him
always moving to another phase

In the shadow of the mountain
he found bits of love but couldn't stay
a home or promises wouldn't keep him
nor things that people, to him, would say

In the shadow of the mountain
he built his life near the river's bend
lived each day in hopes and searching
never sure his searching would ever end

In the shadow of the mountain
he controlled his patience night and day
but soon his restlessness would find him
then one early morning he drifted away

In the shadow of the mountain
as the buds of spring appear
those that knew him held the memory
of his dreams held in a lonely sphere

Of a boy who touched the sunlight
cradled love within his hands
wanting only to love people
in his vast enchanted land

The First Snowfall

This morning I awoke earlier than usual for some unknown reason, sat up in bed and looked out the window to see what kind of day it was going to be. What to my amazement should appear but a snow dressed wonderland. I guess that's why I must have awakened so early, not to miss any of this special day. I quickly got dressed and went outside to explore this most welcome of visits from the heavens.

I saw the slender branches of the maple trees holding many little snow puffs. The cedar and hemlock trees were laden with large patches of white powder, their branches bowing to the audience of nature. Even some of the rust and yellow leaves of the vine maple held their autumn hue, peeking their faces out from their new environment; a thousand smiles everywhere I went.

It was early and as of yet there were neither tire tracks nor footprints, except mine. I felt sad as I walked down the road marring the smooth untouched surface of the snow.

Flakes were floating down from the clouds, landing on my nose, my cheeks, my eyelashes as I looked upward, thanking my creator for this wonderful experience, and for my eyes to see and my skin to feel sensations and my ears, to hear the earth and my nose to smell life's growth and my heart to feel happy.

A New Part of Life

The sun is disappearing behind the trees across the river and the shadows are getting long. There is a playful breeze coming through the open door behind me. It is a good feeling sitting here in my mountain home writing this to you.

When you come to visit me I can now share a more meaningful world with you, for I have learned more of myself from my new environment, and now must live that life feeling new growth. Living in nature has caused me to look into myself for the many answers to the many questions I have looked to man to answer for me. From man I received only answers that could not satisfy the feeling of truth that my soul demanded.

So the new parts of me you will have to get to know for they will be strange to you as you knew me before. Allow time to mellow this unknown portion of me and you will find comfort and security in my words and actions. Your understanding of me will bring us closer together.

As we change from the brush strokes of encounters, my friend, we blend into a canvas of the world the great artist imagined.

Learning From You

I want to learn from you by becoming a part of your life. Within your eyes I see mirrored many experiences which have given you insight into yourself, channels I wish also to explore. By being yourself you show me all the things I wish to be but am not.

Life's music began
as the puppet walked upon the stage
held by the master's hands
do what I command, my little wooden
    friend
the puppeteer grunted
I gave you life
and by these strings
only shall you live

The Puppet

when the audience
finds you tiresome
I will cut your strings
and discard you
to the pile of trash
for I will need you no more
so be of good use to me
as you live
that coins shall
jingle in my pocket

now a puppet is a puppet
    and a puppet has no choice
but you, my friend are human
    and with this you can rejoice

The cry of your spirit
echoed through the strains
as your fingers picked the
strings of your heart
running the fields
with you
we threw our dreams
to the wind
as night's shroud
protected our serenity
deeper we plunged
into each other
our shells becoming
transparent rays of the sun
your music rolled toward me
coming to rest
within me
like the waves crashing
with thunderous energy
to rest in the arms of the sand
    ... this is called love!

The Capacity of Love

The capacity of love is only stifled
by our lack of experience
as the bird who sits in the nest
until it learns to fly
one of our greatest joys
is to be a new experience
to another person ... for love
has many faces

Your existence no longer has to be justified,
nor do those feelings you hold inside, either
to yourself or to others. Just your striving to
live, the focus being your true self through
much of your life may seem out of focus, is
justification.

                    ... without explanation

Become Rich

You may be poor in possessions
but you can become rich in your
ability to experience the essence of life

possessions get old
break
wear out
time weakens their use
and are many times discarded
but the experience of love
is a person's greatest asset
which endures the years.

Many Ways to Learn

Friendship becomes deep when virtuous men learn to love the good in one another and understand the bad which clutters the mind ... for virtue gives more joy than the physical plane of beauty, being untouched by time.

You Lifted Me

Naked with only nature's cover
I was lifted above the earth
you carrying me toward the water
as the waves ran to meet us
our warm skin rubbing with
a sensual softness
your muscles in rhythm
to your purpose
a protective coating
for the long journey
as you walked on top
of the water's crest
I rested my cheek
under the curvature
of your chin, calm,
knowing your footsteps
would lead us
to a place beyond
where creating love
was the reason
for our journey

Love Is Not A Sound

Love is not a sound
often times spoken in haste
or promises you intend not to keep
or a walk down a one way street

Love is hope where hope was once severed
    from your mind
Love is living each moment with the person
    of love you find
Love is trust when trust repeatedly stole
    from your life
Love is never giving up when you're
  despondent
        or in strife
Love is seeing all you can
in each and every man
'tis not a sound
that makes love profound

I Come

You are the night
I am the sun
I chose to walk
you chose to run
you are the millions
I am but one
I search for love
you offer fun
I give my heart
you disclose none
you are tall buildings
between them I come
you are the night
I am the sun

Learning to Love

To the Mother of Nature was born a child
        naked to man thoughts
and she wrapped him in innocence
        for mankind was cruel
and she nursed him with compassion
        for mankind was harsh
and the child suckled from her breasts
        of kindness and goodness
        for mankind was selfish
and he began to grow and to learn
and his feet began to feel the humid soil
and his hands began to feel his sensitive
    body
and his eyes began to see the wonder of
            living things
and his ears began to hear the harmonious
    sounds
            of the creatures
and his nose began to smell the aroma of
    life

134

and he was curious
and he started to roam
and he started to explore
and he started to absorb
and he became involved
and he grew and he learned
and Mother Nature watched with great pride
and he felt the thorns of the berry bushes
    from which he ate
and he felt the sting of the bee from which
    he obtained honey
and he felt the sharp edges of broken
  branches
    of the trees he used to build his home
and he felt the pain of fire, when touched, he
    used for warmth
and he felt the discomfort of certain plants
    from which he sought to derive food
and he learned to respect all forms of life
and he learned what not to touch
and he learned what was not good for him
and he learned to be careful yet not afraid
and he learned the difference of each
and he felt good

and he learned and he grew
and he began to see himself as part of all
   he saw
and he took from life only what he needed
and he took from life only what was good
and he became a part of the balance
and he cared about all he saw
and he grew and he learned
and he helped the weaker in Nature
and he honored the stronger in Nature
and he saw life and death in harmony
and he knew he was being taught
and he saw continuity
and he saw simplicity
and he saw humility
and he saw wisdom
and he learned and he grew
and he saw families of things
and he saw them caring about each other
and he saw them sharing with each other
and he saw them fulfilling their purpose
and he began to look for his own kind
and he began to yearn for a family

and he grew and he learned
and he searched
and he experienced
and he contemplated
and one day he found his own kind
and he wanted to relate
and he entered his family in innocence
and he gave of himself with compassion
and he was filled with kindness and goodness
and he communicated in a language called
   love
and his body was motivated by the expression
        of love
and he told his people how he had learned
and he was spontaneous in love
and he was deliberate in love
and how he appeared to be what he was
and how he had grown from the guidance
     of his Mother, Nature
and his family thought him strange
and his family thought him different
and he asked ... was there any other way to be!

City Dwellers

Your first responsibility is to yourself
tend to your own body
    that it may serve you well
tend to your own mind
    that it may take you beyond
then offer your imagination as a gift
your knowledge as a lesson
your wisdom as a virtue
    without obligation
    without reward
    without restitution

that our youth may become
the living statues sculpted for a
    better world

My Attic

'Tis not for you I shed my tears
but for that part of me
that always is alone
when my eyes are dry
all those forgotten people
whom I loved
are put back on the dusty shelves
of memories
my attic that created tears
the door once more closed
until another time
where thought and deed
leads up the stairs to
tears of things
that passed me by
someday, no more
will enter that cobwebbed room
where sorrow is the air I breathe
and torment my only light

Yesterday

Do your eyes betray
the sad and lonely times
of yesterday
when one small word
hello!
could have replaced the sorrow
with a smile upon your face

sensitive love
could have lifted your body
from the blacktop streets
the carnival buildings
those fickle signs
promising thrills and chances
substitutes for love

one night of affection
might have soothed
your longing
until another time
your feet are tired
the cold wind
forces you inside
to a bed of isolation

tomorrow is another day
should you awake
with joyful eyes
in hopes that love
will come a calling
with but a simple word
hello!

Danny

Grew up with mother and brother on a
        ranch in California
they scratched the land for subsistence
poor in possessions ... rich in health and
        simplicity
the boy of seventeen I met was a wild youth
        abounding with endless energy
        challenging life at every opportunity
        every animal, every blade of grass
            was his friend
for the first time he came to the city
        living with me for many months
the city became confusing, cluttered
people's words and motives became hurts he
            didn't understand
his innocence was challenged
he began to question my kindness, my love
        when men of folly would interpret to
            him my motives as a lie

so he ran away, back to the country, to the
        trees and stream and animals he knew
a few years later I saw him again in his
        environment and he spoke these
                words to me

In your city I became a slave to man's greed
and was overwhelmed by his flattery and
lustful persuasion and did not hear the
voice of my soul and still with all the pain I
caused, you came back as my friend. Will
you stay that I may learn your ways? It
seems our voices within are the same.

You, My City

How you pull me apart with your instability, with your inconsistency for I never know what your moods will be from day to day. You never will make a commitment that we might build together. Sometimes you surround me with affection and other times with indifference, as if you don't know me. I can take your hurting me, I can take the struggles, I can endure the pain but I cannot take your indifference.

For three years I have been courting you, trying to develop a relationship whereby I cared to stay. Maybe we could even live together building a home, a family of people. But time has shown me you are fickle with many lovers and you chose me when your need arose, not concerned that I had needs also—that I might want to plant

144

roots and belong to your family, even though I be only one of your lovers. I accepted that fate.

You teased me when I first met you and promised things you could not fulfill. It took all this time for me to realize ... Love was a game in which you made up the rules to suit your purpose. When I couldn't play you ignored me. I still tried for I loved you, with hope, with devotion, and gave all I knew of myself and then gave what I newly learned from you. Still it was not enough.

So I am leaving you, maybe forever, maybe for awhile. I must travel to other places where I may find civilization in need of what life has made of me.

What It Is to Be Human

I am sitting in the Portland Greyhound bus terminal, having a cup of coffee. Coffee is the remembrance, for me, of years gone by. The nectar of the gods afforded strangers for the time when all other words fail their lips. The hour is 10:30 at night. Darkness seems the time when the attic of one's mind is visited in search of some lost treasure, forgotten, as a lost love revived to what may have been, but wasn't. Outside the rain is pouring from the clouds like tears from love when it is alone. How sad is the rain tonight or maybe the rain is laughing tears of joy. I guess it depends where you are or where you have been.

A couple of hours ago I was sitting in my home up in the mountains, listening to the music of my past, within the comforts of my bedroom. The familiar things one collects over the years to keep reminding us of what once was. Gifts from people to bridge the heart. As I lay on my bed the music began to bring back memories of people and places I used to know. My thoughts became a cavern where the echos of the past bounced against every wall and ceiling of my mind. Faster and deeper came the penetration until the reality of the now became the reliving of the many yesterdays where hopes and dreams were the lights I followed from the blackness, where my feelings could not relate to the reality surrounding me or my heartbeat be heard by those close to me. Only in the distance of time was my soul illuminated, seeing the white peaks of truth as clear as crystal.

… people who stole my time, absorbed my knowledge, experimented with my being, syphoned my generosity, then disappeared into the mass of humanity, becoming the past that, on lonely nights such as this, would cause my restlessness to increase its search for whatever would still my flesh and bones to a quiet bed of understanding; people who said they loved me meaning they were in love with the idea of being in love; people who used my friendship, my companionship to kill time instead of time to live; people who thought sex was love and bed was home; people who gave to me because they believed in what I was trying to make of my life; people who loved me as I was without trying to change me; people who gave love to me from the feelings of their heart not the lust of their minds; people who truly wanted to become a part of my life; people who wanted to increase their capacity to love and were willing to step into the unknown with me; people who were not afraid to show you they cared; people who gave more of themselves in a few encounters than most can in years. ... people I picked out of the gutter of life; people I held when no one else cared; people I sat with when the world was spinning around them; people I took from the cold indifferent city streets and warmed their bodies and their minds in my home; people who had given up on life until I gave them a reason to care, a motivation, a purpose to continue; people who carried weapons of pain I substituted with tools of love; people in whose faces I always saw the image of love and myself falling in love with those faces over and over again until my world became a forest of faces with blond hair, black hair, a face with sad eyes, a face with a straight nose, a face with a scar, a face with a square chin, a face with bright cheeks, a face with a beard, a face with soft skin, a face with sensitive eyes, a face of strength, of compassion, of classical beauty, of simple thoughts.

... Faces I wanted to give love to, minds I wanted to enter, bodies I wanted to explore bringing them the riches of touch and affection beyond their imagination that would make gold crumble to dust, jewels become as dull as a gray sky.

... becoming one as the romantic rhythm of the sea, the poetic words of the soul, the rebirth of the human spirit.

Places with high mountains, desert sands, miles of ocean beaches, pine and cedar forests, groves of cyprus trees, rose garden backyards, tulip beds and morning glory fences, an old swing on a wooden front porch, a park on a summer night, a haystack in a barnyard, a campfire by a lake, a cabin by highway 101, a basement of a Victorian house in San Francisco, a Y.M.C.A. room in Phoenix, an apartment in Dallas, a barn in northern California, a house in Pittsburgh, a room in Portland, a trailer in Los Angeles, a hotel in Tulsa, a camper in Maine, a street in New York, a diner in Lexington, a campsite in the redwoods, small towns and large cities, country roads and fast freeways began to merge as one as the flood of memories engulfed the spaces of my mind. The years began to pass like an autumn wind blowing the leaves from the tree of my life until it was stripped bare. I stood naked but the wind kept blowing, bending the branches of my naked soul and for a moment I felt as if I would be uprooted by its force. So I jumped up from the bed and drove the forty miles into Portland hoping to find another face that might still my restless soul. Maybe this time there would be no separation and the memories we would share together.

It has been several hours as I have been sitting here in the bus station writing this. Most of the people who were here when I arrived are gone now, except for the girl with a newborn baby (what kind of world will it find), a lady with a shopping bag whose face mirrored her smiling a lot, a young man wearing an army uniform which seemed out of place, an old man who misplaced his hat and overcoat but later found them, and a young girl who was sitting alone until a young man asked if he might join her (when she got up to refill her coffee cup he looked at me with a smile for she was very pretty).

How many bus stations have I sat in all over the country. And for how many reasons have I been brought into their domain. Listening to the loudspeaker announcing places where people lived out their lives or at least a part of them. Some to me were a memory and others unknown. Here I am back again, a restless traveler of the universe, who travels on wishes walking upon an illusion that is real, that love, someday, will come to stay. Will reality be so kind as to grant me safe passage through the time barrier?

I have grown from youth to manhood and still, for whatever reason eludes me, my dreams still seem to stay intact. My motivation continues to steer the course of my destiny over the roughest of waters even though the land of hope at times seems far away.

The coffee shop is closing and the next bus doesn't leave till morning. So back out in the city I will head and sometime soon write of times and places and people who become a part of my past, of my feelings, of my learning what it is to be human.

Shenandoah Valley

Blue water winds itself
around autumn's
browns and golds
like the ribbon
of a package
truly it was a gift
given to man
as I wandered down
from the Blue Ridge Mountains
my eyes beheld
this spot of earth
nature has been kind
to this valley
for beauty was abundant
quaint little farms
nestled on the knolls

among the stately trees
naked now
sunshine warming the day
bringing together the colors
in harmonious patterns
clouds, the minstrels of the sky
singing songs of bygone days
the sun rose three times
before I journeyed on
to other places
where people lived out
their lives
I, still searching
for where I belonged

The Piano

I sat in the Harvard University common room listening to the vibrant music of my friend as he played the grand piano; sounds pirouetting back and forth, touching the high walnut ceiling and carved wooden walls, waltzing in and out of the arched windows. The black silhouetted trees stood motionless outside listening to his performance.

The music he played paralleled the grandeur of the old ornate furniture which stood within the room, telling of times and relationships and of young men who would find greatness beyond this school of learning, who sat in these very chairs listening to their friend playing the piano, as I was at that very moment. Paintings hanging on the walls created by well-known artists of their times, of men who have contributed to the growth and destiny of our lives.

I felt I was reliving history, my imagination running rampant with the events that happened here on these grounds. Young men who felt the same enchantment and inspiration I was feeling as my friend echoed the great composers, my mood being changed by Bach, Beethoven, Strauss, Brahms as they spoke of their lives and loves. An aura of people of past and present completing the now as I lived each timeless moment.

My friend, his long curly blond hair, white turtleneck sweater, construction boots and maroon pants with a hole in the knee making his feelings known; a long-haired hippie sitting at the grand piano at Harvard University playing for me what his lips could not speak or his body accept, only in the communication his fingers manifested as they ran over the keys sounding through the great halls of this university on one summer night in June.

Reflections

I am what I am as my past reflects
what life has chiseled me
just as this rock's fragments fall
from the pounding of the relentless sea

There's a time to act, a time to dream
and a time to understand
that nothing ever stays the same
neither rock, nor shore, nor man

Someday the rock will be no more
someday I too will cease
but not before I build my dream
then my soul, can be released

When Love Arrives

I want to be unattached
from mankind's inability
to give from the soul
free from man's restraints
I wish
to recapture my own soul
my youthful dreams
to make love to you
to make love to people
to make love to the world

feel the sand between my toes
the sun at my fingertips
the clouds in my hair
the flowers in my eyes
the wind in my veins
the summer meadows in my heart

feel the hands of love
upon my skin
feel the sensual beauty of love
when love arrives

A Long Journey

I am very tired and weak from my long
   journey
Would you carry my belongings for awhile!
I have not much, just a broken heart that I
will have to mend, a cloak of courage
that is worn and dusty that I will need to
cleanse, and my boots of hope that have
   protected
my footsteps through life's brambles which
   need resoling
May I rest within your home a short while
   to do
those mentioned things before I start on my
journey's way?

Written To A Friend

Don't run away
because you expect from me
that which is you
your small world
can become overcrowded
feelings need space to grow
let our world expand
without boundaries
without fences
without cement fortresses
without those substitutes
which detain our participating
in this expansion

I would rather hurt you myself, in your learning from me of life and love, than see someone or something else crush your will to live.

Condemnation

Be hesitant in your condemnation
   of others
as their charity creates within you
               expectations
as their love creates within you
               animosity
as their presumptions create within you
               suspicion
as their interpretation creates within you
               disbelief
as their spontaneity creates within you
               fear
what they feel is not man-made judgments
only the soul can understand the soul
         ... children know!

Friend Or Lover

Should I try to love you
as we be lovers
and if love fails
will we grow away from each other
or should I stay and accept
the pieces and parts that are together
as in friendship
in hopes someday
they may become whole
rather than take the chance
of starting all over again
with someone else
later finding
we didn't try hard enough
now the pieces have scattered
we have stood too long
on the desert of
being alone

That I May Know Of You

Stranger
    to the life I've lived
stranger
    to the love I'd gladly give
yes speak, oh speak ... speak
    make that lovely sound
    that I may know of you

stranger
    speak a gentle phrase or two
stranger
    I will stop to answer you
yes speak, oh speak ... speak
    make that lovely sound
    that I may know of you

stranger
    talk of love and love will surely stay
stranger
    talk of fear and I will send it far away
yes speak, oh speak … speak
    make that lovely sound
    that I may know of you

stranger
    say your needs that they freely may be
               known
stranger
    and I will fill those needs as they,
           to me are shown
yes speak, oh speak … speak
    make that lovely sound
    that I may know of you

Words

There was a time when I believed in all words. This time being when I was young. I would listen, believing. Over the years my ears have become calloused and somewhat deaf to the words, false to the heart from which they spoke. I cried, often in silence from the hurts. But the wounds would soon heal, the scab disappears, leaving only a scar to remind me. Now I listen with my eyes.

Sitting by the banks of the Sandy River early this fall morning, when the sun was still behind the ridge—my friend was looking out over the waters—I watching his face becoming more distinguishable as dawn approached realizing as I watch that face ...

    It isn't who you love
    or how you love
    It's just that you love

Poets, Who Will Come After Him

His legacy found its roots in the poems his heart had created. When flesh and bones vanish, as life demands, what will be said of him. Will poets speak praise upon their lips of a man who was the shepherd of love or judge him a fool who lived in dreams sitting upon the clouds? Will the poets who come after him be inspired by his legacy or laugh in dismay at his trite and simple words? Maybe some will say he cared to give all he knew, but his being different was not the common, ordinary thing to do. That he was crucified by his own truth.

Is he dead? ask the poets of tomorrow!

If I can feel secure in my changes
then I know life can truly become exciting

If words lead to actions
then you must learn to speak your feelings

Trust in feelings
they are the voices of our soul

Many people ask the question, why?
but not enough make the statement, why not!

THE
HUMANNESS
OF YOU

A Day's Adventure

I sat on a small fence in a redwood grove (Richardsons Grove State Park) in Northern California one early morning in late June. The rays of the sun were just beginning to penetrate the trees. The birds had started to talk of the coming day, and the wind began to stir, swaying the branches as it moved through the grove.

This had always been one of my favorite spots when travelling along the Pacific Coast, which I did frequently. This time I was alone, and I wanted to let things happen without instigating them. I felt at peace with myself, watching and listening to life wake up to the most beautiful days.

A short time passed, and I heard soft footsteps on the carpet of pine needles and looked up to see a young girl walking my way. She said "good morning" with a warm smile and sat down beside me. We shared time talking of our lives, what love meant to us, our dreams, wondering if we'd have the time or strength to see them through. She believed we did. That made me feel good. I watched her get up to go and kissed her on the cheek. She then took my hand and we embraced saying in silence what could not be said in words. In a moment she was lost among the giant trees.

A while later a young boy rode by on a bicycle, smiling as he waved hello. His face showed no hate, no fear. His long blond hair and tanned body looked like he was born of the sun, a messenger from the universe.

I strolled down to the river helping two little children catch some baby trout that were in a small pool. We tried for some time but they were too fast for us. Even their parents helped, and we all laughed. It was fun being together with strangers who became friends.

The Eel River seemed very warm as my feet walked over its rocky bottom. I stopped, looking up at the top of the redwood trees, and for a few minutes deeply thought of the perfect harmony of nature and that I wanted to be a part of that harmony.

A young boy about sixteen years old came up and asked if I'd like to go swimming with him. We swam and floated down the river and dove in a deep pool. We splashed water at each other and skipped rocks across the water and then rested upon the earth. We talked of his friends and their search for new values, new ways of living, for their own identity. We both were very open with each other in our thoughts and feelings. We related for several hours then he had to go. The last words he said were, "I wish I had known you when I was growing up."

The whole day was filled with inter-actions of people. The inspiration of friendliness and touching by these human beings filled my heart with hope, that there is a new beginning. There was no fear.

Life flowed as it should on this exceptional day.

Faces Of Life

No matter where the highway leads me
no matter where I roam
faces in
a hundred places
drifting in and out of towns, alone

I take the time to share my kisses
to touch a cheek that's tan
their endless dreams
that always seem
to shift through years of changing sand

A face beside a roadside diner
a face beneath a tree
a friendly smile
says stay awhile
is a face that looks intuitively

A face beside a lighted lamppost
searching for a warm embrace
those lonesome eyes
those desperate cries
is a face without a special place

A face whose beauty swells the senses
churns the feeling of the heart
your soul ignites
emotions flight
is the face the seed of oneness starts

A face held by the morning sunshine
youth's face, tenderly bound
a moment's chance
bares a glance
in shyness, expressing to be found

So faces of my travelled highway
let me love you while I may
I am caring
need your sharing
don't let this precious moment stray.

The world is full of
             wonders
I know because they
have made themselves
known to me.

A person cannot develop
the full extent of his
mind and body unless
his home and surroundings
are in harmony
with his feelings.

Search for this harmony.

Do we give love for giving?
Do we receive love for receiving?
Or are we love
as a flower's fragrance, just is.
Not concerned with a receiver
or a giver.
Just is.

Let us become love.
Let us be love.

Life Will Unfold To You

Rain clouds teasing the summer's sun
winter playing hide and seek with spring
warm breezes heralding summer's approach
autumn the jester of the seasons

people walking upon the earth's crust
where mountains unknown push above
the ocean's surface
where volcanoes unleash the power
of the earth's core
where lands give birth to new worlds
and love is the air you breathe
life will unfold

Being Taught

White birch standing in torrents of rain
an old two-story southern house, proud at
watching history unfold
a squirrel scurrying across the house's red tile
roof.
Lightning seen as a memory—thunder heard
clouds, oranged, streaked turning across the
sky like the pages of a great book.
My eyes looking upward, downward, scanning
everywhere as if trying to penetrate the
obvious for a deeper meaning. As I wrote what I
observed and felt, the meaning became simple.
I was being taught.

"I Want To Be Happy"

To share life with the meadows,
to smell the tide beneath my feet,
to climb the hills or run upon the valleys floor,
to watch the little creatures make their day,
to see the birth of flowers
and above birds soaring with graceful ease,
to sense the sun upon my body
and feel the rain upon natures brow,
listen to the melody of the stream
and the wind running through the branches,
the lark to wake me from my sleep
and the owl to bid me good night
            with you beside me.

Messenger Of Wisdom

Once appeared a wise man, though a
      stranger in my dreams
he came upon a chariot riding down the
      sun-lit beams
pulled by celestial horses who grazed
      the milky way.
He held the reins of wisdom, in my sight he'll
      always stay
his words they echoed loud across the
      vastness of the sky
only once, would he share my world,
      this his passing by
he took me in his chariot and talked
      of many things
showed me worlds beyond my dreams that
      would astonish even kings
he said my son these dreams you see are
      all within your grasp
if you continue searching and take the
      time to ask.

Teacher Of Life

One morning, beneath a spring sun, beside
the gnarled limbs of an old tree, sat an
old man whose white garment flowed as
the wind arose then settled peacefully
upon his body. His eyes wandered slowly
over the countryside, then came to rest
upon the white marble pillars
near the city gates.

The group of young people that surrounded
him were silent, waiting impatiently for
his words. Looking into his eyes they saw
the universe. Each in their own image.
Each felt the space and time
of their dreams.

Presently, the man's attention focused upon
one particular youth and the man began to
speak;

"In all my years I have searched for a man
wiser than myself, yet this man I have not
yet found.

Those that thought themselves wise kindled
their wisdom with false pride and ignorance
           I listened

Those that spoke truth within the limits
of their heart did not perceive themselves
to be wise

           I respected
Those who made love visible in their daily toil
thinking not of becoming wise
           I admired."

Love Me

Love me | because I try to touch life within the framework of uncertainty

love me | in the shadows of my indecisions as I strive to gain knowledge

love me | in the silence of my hurts and the noise of my confusions

love me | for the feeling of my heart not the fears of my mind

love me | in my search for truth though I may stumble upon fallacy

love me | as I pursue my dreams sometimes retarded by illusions

love me   as I grow to know myself
even during the times of
stagnation

love me   because I seek harmony
not man's discord

love me   for my body that I wish to
share with affection,
wrapping you in warmth

love me   because we are different
as we are the same

love me   that our time together will
be spent in growing, kindling
the world with understanding

love me   not with expectations
but with hope

I will love you the same.

Feel and see things
　　　you've never felt before

Ride the seed as it is carried
　　　by the wind

to unknown places,
　　　unknown faces

For it will settle somewhere
　　　upon a spot of earth

And fulfill its purpose.

To Understand

To be alone, yet not lonely
to be hurt, yet to love
to feel fear, yet not be afraid
to feel change, yet not confusion
　　　is to understand.

Human Affection

Sometimes there is no philosophy
    or words to help you
when you're drowning in hurts,
    suffocating in struggle.
So I will jump in and take hold
    of you in silence.
Touch you with my hands.

The most sensitive expression,
    the deepest single communication
of emotion, of feelings, between
    two people is when the mind and
body express as one.
    This we call affection.
It becomes a positive force,
    directed toward the growth
of greater understanding and intimacy.

Affection, expressed openly, is good.
    It eliminates emotional fears,
    frees emotional desires.

Poetry Of Light

I

When you give do not expect
a giving in return
just give because you feel it
then happiness you will earn

II

When I become aware of your needs, trying
to fulfill them, many of my own are at peace.

III

Let your body love
before your intellect controls

IV

To be human
you have to chance
being hurt.

Need For Solitude

I wanted so much to get away
from my city and its people.
Go out into the countryside
and unwind.
This morning I went skinny-dipping
at Cherry Creek.
The water was so warm
and it was ever so quiet.
Once in a while a child
would laugh out loud
while playing in the water
but other than that I only heard
the sounds of birds and the splashing water
and my own breathing.
The sun wrapped its arms around me
and the wind played with my hair.

> We don't need loud music
>   or the sound of motors
>   or the hum of cities
>   or crowds of people
>   to feel secure.

Experience

Have you felt a grain of sand
　　　and given it meaning

Have you planted a speck of earth
　　　and harvested love

Have you taken a blade of grass
　　　and listened to it grow

Have you travelled with a bee
　　　sharing its journey

Have you walked the thread
　　　of a spider's web

Have you watched a blossom
　　　turn into a cherry

Have you sat upon a mountain top
　　　seeing the wonderment of earth

If you have, you've begun to see
　　　the reason for it all

To The Children

I'll bring you a sky full of blue birds
I'll compose you a rhyme to enjoy
I'll cool your cheeks with a mountain stream
and we'll play with the clouds as our toys

I'll show you the frost in the morning
I'll lead you by day with the sun
I'll guide you to new worlds in the forest
where you can dance and sing and run

I'll share all the trees and wild flowers
all the creatures of this speck of earth
I'll teach you that difference is together
that all love is a part of your birth

"Vision"
(at the Battleground of Antietam, Virginia)

Once there was a cornfield
on a farm near yonder woods
stalks grew strong and golden
as against the sky they stood

farmers working with their plows
lush trees upon the hills
a countryside abundant
from man's sweat, the soil he tilled

the earth began to quiver
twelve thousand men in grey
were marching toward this cornfield
to meet the blue next day

preparations for the battle
were pursued by both the sides
the grey dug earthen trenches
so from bullets they could hide

next morning in the early dawn
the battle had begun

before the ears of ripening corn
felt the warmth of summer's sun

through the field the men in blue
charged toward the line of gray
as smoke and powder filled the air
the generals watched and prayed

stalks of corn began to fall
with every bullet's thrust
for men and corn became both one
as they fell upon the dust

back and forth the battle raged
on who possessed the field
the blue had it several times
but always had to yield

finally when the darkness came
a peace encased the land
a dying stalk of corn would
represent the body of a man

I gaze upon this solemn place
with fearful eyes I see
a vision of a corn stalk
that my son, someday, might be.

If This Were Your Last Day My Son

If this were your last day my son,
would you walk upon the sea
to finds the lands beyond your birth
you dreamed someday that you would see.

If this were your last day, my son,
would you write upon the sand
a poem of love your thoughts encased
as death awaits to take your hand.

If this were your last day, my son,
would you see your mother's face
baking cookies in the kitchen
or patching Levi's by the fireplace.

If this were your last day, my son,
would you say to all of man
I'll die not again to propogate
a war, where you have made your stand.

This Speck Of Earth

The man stopped, wiped his brow, scratched his ear, picked up a stick, raised his head to look about and saw the long furrows of his planting. Through the branches he looked up toward the sunny sky and saw the rain clouds drifting in from the north for it was time, the earth was thirsty.

His head turned toward the hills—their cover of grain, shortly, would be ready to harvest— then followed the row of trees to where his cabin sat—thinking of the time when the trees were cut, then seasoned, so the walls would be strong and sturdy.

Then his eyes followed the river as it wound itself around the valley and he remembered as a youth the many times the river had wound itself around his life. He never felt alone in this land nor would his family.

My Brothers

Yes, my brothers, I can love you
not just the love within your mind
but also the love your body can give

what meaning has the body
    without a good mind to rule it
what meaning has the mind
    without a body to illuminate it

Those Wonderful People

All the rich and joy-filled moments we shared together and the times of solitude we also needed to digest the fullness of human happiness.

The times when our lack of understanding caused us hurt only to be resolved by the security of our love.

Not a day passed in my childhood and youth that you didn't find some way to give even when you were tired or carried a troubled heart.

From you I learned charity and compassion and tolerance. From you I learned to like myself.

I feel your image as a part of me, your lessons mirrored by my deeds.

Mom & Dad, if I suffer or am lonely or feel hurts, it is not because of you, but only that you opened me to so much love I have not yet found a world to give it all to.

Justice ...?

The army ...   gave a man a medal for
                   killing another man, and
                   a dishonorable discharge
                   for loving one

the state ...   awarded a man an honor
                   for arresting men as
                   criminals, and put him in
                   prison for the criminal
                   act of loving one

the church ...   praised a man for loving
                   mankind, then
                   condemned him for
                   loving a man

people ...   respect a man's capacity
                   to speak of love, until he
                   seeks to manifest his
                   words

I Understand

I understand I must love myself
   before I can love others.

I understand I must be open
   so I can open others unto themselves.

I understand I must be honest
   if I expect that of my friend.

I understand I must speak the truth
   if I am to hear the truth spoken.

I understand that I must reach out to people
   if I am to be touched.

I understand I must share
   if I am to be given.

I understand my knowledge must be used
   if I am to grow.

I understand you must have freedom
   if I am to be free.

Lend Me

Lend me room to expand and to grow
Lend me a home where love I can know
Lend me a touch so I can feel
Lend me your time so my hurts can heal
Lend me the freedom to love all men
Lend me the courage to try again and again
I'll give to you a human being whose only
    intent
Is building life on what you have lent.

Learning Love

I want to learn to love,
It's not something you can teach me,
but it's something I can learn from you,
you inspire me
when you tell me how beautiful I am,
that you love me
and you project love also
I begin to look into myself as to why—
you show me myself by being you
I've known you but a short time,
but I trust you—
its a feeling you've given me,
I want to learn by being around you;
Sometimes I feel I want to be
around you forever,
then I realize, as you have told me, that
you're just a stepping stone in my life,
so for me to learn I must not hold back,
help me to learn not to hold back,
help me to learn to love.

"Human Potential"

In the time we were together he asked nothing from me beyond a kiss and our embracing one another. I understood him, that he wanted me to know his love was from his soul, not just his body.

I felt comfortable in his company and only wanted to possess what would increase his happiness. I felt a time would come when our bodies would merge as one and our minds would explore, together, the vast reserve of human potential.

A Man

A man ... acts with honor and pride
               yet bends to gather food
for friends in their hunger

a man ... walks naked
               in the forest of his people
so they may see his truth ...

a man ... touches all of life
               for he is not afraid
to extend himself

a man's ... work in his labors
               shows his love for living

a man ... is strong and self-confident
               yet his eyes may sparkle
               with rain drops

a man ... projects the excitement and
               wonderment of a child
               the experience and
               understanding of an adult
               upon the screen of life
youth is his audience

If You Lose

If you lose faith in people
    you've lost your chance of sharing
        then someone becomes lonely, besides
            you

If you lose confidence in yourself
    you've lost your reason of motivation
    then others must supply a vehicle
    if they don't you become stagnant

If you lose consideration of others
    you've lost the respect of yourself
        then ugliness spreads

If you lose your sense of involvement to a
    cause or ideal
        you've lost the expansion of your soul
        our world becomes less

If you lose your willingness to labor
   you've lost the growth of yourself
      then you become a leech

If you lose your own thoughts
   you've lost the freedom not to become a
      slave
         you create more masters
      then I must fight harder to maintain
         my freedom

If you lose your sense of wonderment, of
   exploring
      of experiencing
   you've lost the miracle of learning
   then ignorance runs rampant

If you become indifferent
   you've lost
      we all suffer

Children Of The Night

You—oh desert town
dressed
with desert palms
cactus gardens
and desert winds blow
sand across the desert cover
of your streets
money walls of brick and stone
secure your people
mortared objects
hold your thoughts—in place
pools of gold and silver
caress your appetites
lighted signs, your lamp posts
confuse the serenity
of your star-filled night

darkness empties your
busy streets, crowded sidewalks

your people retiring
to their rich, abundant
materialistic Gods

Each and every night
from the shadows, emerge
the children of the streets
"street people"
whose short lives
have woven a precious cloak
of warm, protecting fibers
for your displaced youth
who have wandered
to your warm and sunny days
Oh desert town
those whose difference
is distasteful to your kind
those youth whose hardships
is beyond your caring

of lives abused
in body and in mind
of lives whose splints
hold the broken trust
and broken hearts and broken homes

and broken hope
none the less
they find a way
to fill the empty gaps
and find a meaning to their
endless wanderings

by accepting, their differences
as a bond
traveling towns and cities
contemplating
somewhere, sometime
a feeling of belonging

stopping long enough, to build
or reconstruct a reason
to continue searching
for the balance
as a way of life

This special night
four of them came together
this destiny proclaimed
under the cover of
a single palm tree

four lives in timeless
awaking or reawaking
shattering barriers
into fragments
souls released
in exploration
four youths
standing before a shattered world
beginning to understand
that difference must be shown
through experience, only, is it known
that truth a weapon of the soul
is fought with love
not sword nor twisted tongue
to cut the pieces from the whole

Oh desert town
you tolerate their existence
but if you had the time
or the will of action
to alleviate their presence
on your streets
which mar your image
you would indeed

They no more
could bring to life
the desert nights
as minstrels or story tellers,
with songs of traveled highways
vagabonds of God
they the only people to say
"Hello" and volunteer their
time to me a lonely
stranger to your town.
Your street people
are more real
in searching for truth
than all of you
whose security is
behind your doors
with lock and key

one soul cried tears of happiness
upon being born again
one soul enhanced a vision
of himself
one soul realized, in clear thoughts,

her true desires
one soul torn away at the protective
coating of his feelings
then ran away for fear
it was not enough
and would be taken away
as all else had
he loved

they parted
not the same
as before they met
but with renewed
purpose and direction
realizing
clouds of despair
may often cover
the warming rays of joy

One Of A Kind

You
unique
a wonderful addition to life
   for there is no one else like you

you are important
believe it ... know it
allow your realization
to radiate among
your fellow man
   for there is no one else like you

reflect your feelings
your hopes ... your dreams
you have much to contribute
take your time
don't hurry
tomorrow will wait for you
   for there is no one else like you

grow with your difference
be proud ... be happy
like yourself
become a new experience
for other people
they can learn from you
     for there is no one else like you

the world needs you
when you hold back
the world is that much less
     for there is no one like you.

May this night find you at peace with yourself. Close your eyes and in your sleep, this night, dream once more of finding love and a way of life. For tomorrow begins another unknown journey into the world of a new day.

Allow people to know of you
of your humanness.

This is not the end—but a new beginning. I am not afraid anymore in the dawn of a new day for I have felt the humanness of you.

And of myself!

Please feel free to write me of your feelings, your reactions to my poetry. We all need to express ourselves. Through the expression of others, we learn about ourselves.

Write to *Walter Rinder*
c/o Celestial Arts
P.O. Box 7123
Berkeley, California 94707

This Page is for You

CW00688647

BOOKS BY DAVID WHYTE

POETRY

Songs for Coming Home
Where Many Rivers Meet
Fire in the Earth
The House of Belonging
Everything is Waiting for You
River Flow: New and Selected Poems
Pilgrim
The Sea in You

PROSE

The Heart Aroused:
Poetry and the Preservation of the Soul
in Corporate America

Crossing the Unknown Sea:
Work as a Pilgrimage of Identity

The Three Marriages:
Reimagining Work, Self and Relationship

Consolations:
The Solace, Nourishment and
Underlying Meaning
of Everyday Words

DAVID WHYTE

Essentials

EDITED BY
GAYLE KAREN
YOUNG WHYTE

20  20

MANY RIVERS PRESS
LANGLEY, WASHINGTON
www.davidwhyte.com

First published in 2020
by Many Rivers Press
PO Box 868
Langley, WA 98260
USA

A catalog record for this book
is available from
the Library of Congress

ISBN 978-1-932887-50-1

Printed in
the United States of America

Reprinted 2020

Nel mezzo del cammin di nostra vita
Mi ritrovai per una selva oscura,
Che la diritta via era smarrita.

In the middle of the road of our life
I awoke in a dark wood,
Where the true way was wholly lost

DANTE ALIGHIERI
The Inferno
Canto 1, line 1
Trans DW

Contents

The act of writing anything worthwhile always takes place at that strange and sometimes disturbing cross-roads where aloneness and intimacy meet. The soli-tariness of the writer, sometimes at a desk, sometimes while writing in a notebook on a skittering knee while travelling, always, if followed rightly, culminates in a radical form of undoing that leads to the distinctions between aloneness and togetherness breaking down altogether. This break of the boundary between what we think is a self and what we think is other than our self is where the rich vein of beauty and insight become a reward in and of itself, and where the words suddenly seem to belong to everyone.

It is all the more satisfying a reward then, to see this essential collection of thoughts and writings, written in so many different circumstances, over so many years, both at home and in so many far places, gathered and brought together by one very close and dear intimate, in the form of my wife and partner, Gayle Karen Young Whyte. It is a double pleasure to have the book designed in collaboration by two very good, very close friends: companions in artistry and in the mountains, Edward Wates and John Neilson. I consider it a great measure of any success in life that those so close to me could remain ardent supporters of the essence of my work over so many years: respect and support always being the neces-sary bedrock of any good marriage or any real friendship.

Speaking of friendship, one of the many ways we have made ourselves lonely without gaining the deeper nourishment and intimacies of true aloneness, is the way we have lost the greater supporting circle of friendship available to us in the created, natural world: to be friends with the sky, the rain, the changing light of a given day and the horizon always leading us beyond the circle we have drawn too readily for ourselves. This book is, in many ways, a celebration of the wider circle of friendship that is our birthright. It is in wishing to deepen and make more intimate, and to live into and up to the consequences of that rich relationship with our world and our astonishing planet, and in posing all the beautiful questions that this world asks of us, that much of this work has been written.

DAVID WHYTE
Langley
August 2019

Start Close In

Start close in,
don't take the second step
or the third,
start with the first
thing
close in,
the step
you don't want to take.

Start with
the ground
you know,
the pale ground
beneath your feet,
your own
way to begin
the conversation.

Start with your own
question,
give up on other
people's questions,
don't let them
smother something
simple.

To hear
another's voice,
follow
your own voice,

wait until
that voice
becomes an
intimate private ear
that can
really listen
to another.

Start right now
take a small step
you can call your own
don't follow
someone else's
heroics, be humble
and focused,
start close in,
don't mistake
that other
for your own.

Start close in,
don't take
the second step
or the third,
start with the first
thing
close in,
the step
you don't want to take.

START CLOSE IN   *This poem was inspired by the first lines of Dante's* Comedia, *written in the midst of the despair of exile from his beloved Florence. It reflects the difficult act we all experience, of trying to make a home in the world again when everything has been taken away; the necessity of stepping bravely again, into what looks now like a dark wood, when the outer world as we know it has disappeared, when the world has to be met and in some ways made again from no outer ground but from the very center of our being. The temptation is to take the second or third step, not the first, to ignore the invitation into the center of our own body, into our grief, to attempt to finesse the grief and the absolutely necessary understanding at the core of the pattern, to forgo the radical and almost miraculous simplification into which we are being invited. Start close in.*

The Journey

Above the mountains
   the geese turn into
      the light again

Painting their
   black silhouettes
      on an open sky.

Sometimes everything
   has to be
      inscribed across
         the heavens

so you can find
   the one line
      already written
         inside you.

Sometimes it takes
   a great sky
      to find that

first, bright
   and indescribable
      wedge of freedom
         in your own heart.

Sometimes with
    the bones of the black
        sticks left when the fire
            has gone out

someone has written
    something new
        in the ashes of your life.

You are not leaving.
    Even as the light fades quickly now,
        you are arriving.

THE JOURNEY *There is every reason to despair due to all the present events that seem out of our control, but there is every reason to hope that with attention and discipline, we can bring ourselves and our societies, through a kind of necessary seasonal disappearance, back into the realm of choice.*

Firstly, the easy part: despair. The world at present seems to be a mirror to many of our worst qualities. We could not have our individual fears and prejudices, our wish to feel superior to others, and our deep desire not to be touched by the heartbreak and vulnerabilities that accompany every life, more finely drawn and better represented in the outer world than are presented to us now, by the iconic and often ugly political figures, encouraging the worst in their fellows that dominate our screens and our times.

Life is fierce and difficult. There is no life we can live without being subject to grief, loss and heartbreak. Half of every conversation is mediated through disappearance. Thus, there is every reason to want to retreat from life, to carry torches that illuminate only our own view, to make enemies of life and of others, to hate what we cannot understand and to keep the world and the people who inhabit it at a distance through prejudicial naming; but therefore, it also follows, that our ability to do the opposite, to meet the other in the world on their own terms, without diminishing them, is one of the necessary signatures of human courage; and one we are being asked to write, above all our flaws and difficulties, across the heavens of this, our present time. The essence in other words of The Journey.

Sweet Darkness

When your eyes are tired,
the world is tired also.

When your vision has gone,
no part of the world can find you.

Time to go into the dark
where the night has eyes
to recognize its own.

There you can be sure
you are not beyond love.

The dark will be your home
tonight.

The night will give you a horizon
further than you can see.

You must learn one thing.
The world was made to be free in.

Give up all the other worlds
except the one to which you belong.

Sometimes it takes darkness and the sweet
confinement of your aloneness
to learn

anything or anyone
that does not bring you alive

is too small for you.

SWEET DARKNESS *This poem was written out of that very physical and almost breathless giving away most human beings feel when they must let go of what seems most precious to them, not knowing how or when it will return, in what form or in what voice - that taking away of the light, walking through divorce or separation, through bereavement or through simply not recognizing the person looking back at us in the mirror. 'Sweet Darkness' was written in a kind of defiant praise of this difficult time of not knowing, a letter of invitation to embrace the beauty of the night and of the foundational human experience of not being able to see, as actually another horizon, and perhaps the only horizon out of which a truly new revelation can emerge. The last line cuts both ways, of course: we ourselves have often helped to make everything and everyone around us far too small, by our lack of faith in the midst of a necessary not knowing, by all the ways we are not holding the conversation.*

Sometimes

Sometimes
if you move carefully
through the forest,

breathing
like the ones
in the old stories,

who could cross
a shimmering bed of leaves
without a sound,

you come
to a place
whose only task

is to trouble you
with tiny
but frightening requests,

conceived out of nowhere
but in this place
beginning to lead everywhere.

Requests to stop what
you are doing right now,
and

to stop what you
are becoming
while you do it,

questions
that can make
or unmake
a life,

questions
that have patiently
waited for you,

questions
that have no right
to go away.

SOMETIMES *Almost all individual and communal transformations take place, especially at the beginning, almost silently, without announcement or declaration that the season and the way forward have changed irrevocably. Like the first falling leaf at the end of summer that goes unnoticed. 'Sometimes' looks at this constant dynamic of entrance through trepidation, anticipation and slowly growing understanding of the new. As a child I was given a lavishly illustrated book of Native American myths and stories, a book I returned to again and again for years, wearing away the edges of the pages as I did, but out of all the haunting stories and intriguing pictures, one stood out for me, the image of a young boy in a primeval forest being taught by an elder how to cross a piece of broken ground, without making a single sound. I returned to this story repeatedly, I know now out of the child's intuition that we are all moving silently and unannounced, all transiting and maturing into new territories and new dispensations without the essentials of those transitions ever having been explained or spoken; the last line in many respects is the essence of the poet's work, to work with the questions 'that have no right to go away' in the life of an individual, in the life of a relationship or marriage, and in our collective conversations in an increasingly fraught, worldwide society.*

The Winter of Listening

No one but me by the fire,
my hands burning
red in the palms while
the night wind carries
everything away outside.

All this petty worry
while the great cloak
of the sky grows dark
and intense
round every living thing.

What is precious
inside us does not
care to be known
by the mind
in ways that diminish
its presence.

What we strive for
in perfection
is not what turns us
into the lit angel
we desire,

what disturbs
and then nourishes
has everything
we need.

What we hate
in ourselves
is what we cannot know
in ourselves but
what is true to the pattern
does not need
to be explained.

Inside everyone
is a great shout of joy
waiting to be born.

Even with the summer
so far off
I feel it grown in me
now and ready
to arrive in the world.

All those years
listening to those
who had
nothing to say.

All those years
forgetting
how everything
has its own voice
to make
itself heard.

All those years
forgetting
how easily
you can belong
to everything
simply by listening.

And the slow
difficulty
of remembering
how everything
is born from
an opposite
and miraculous
otherness.

Silence and winter
have led me to that
otherness.

So let this winter
of listening
be enough
for the new life
I must call my own.

We speak
only with the voices of those
we can hear ourselves

and only for that portion
of the body of the world
it has learned to perceive.

And
here
in the tumult
of the night
I hear the walnut
above the child's swing
swaying its dark limbs
in the wind
and the rain now
come to beat
against my window
and somewhere
in this cold night
of wind and stars
the first whispered
opening of
those hidden
and invisible springs
that uncoil
in the summer air
each yet
to be imagined rose.

THE WINTER OF LISTENING *Within this poem is an ancient intuitive understanding of winter as a time to leave things alone, to let things remain hidden, even to themselves. A time when to name anything would be to give it the wrong name, most especially refusing to name ourselves, a radical sense of letting ourselves alone, without even the most subtle, internal self-bullying or coercion. It is the intimate experience in sitting alone by a fire, in silence and in reverie, with both a simplification and a growing clairvoyance of what is just beginning to be made known. A Winter of Listening.*

The Faces at Braga

In monastery darkness
by the light of one flashlight,
the old shrine room waits in silence.

While above the door
we see the terrible figure,
fierce eyes demanding, 'Will you step through?'

And the old monk leads us,
bent back nudging blackness,
prayer beads in the hand that beckons.

We light the butter lamps
and bow, eyes blinking in the
pungent smoke, look up without a word,

see faces in meditation,
a hundred faces carved above,
eye lines wrinkled in the hand-held light.

Such love in solid wood. Taken from the hillsides
and carved in silence, they have
the vibrant stillness of those who made them.

Engulfed by the past
they have been neglected, but through
smoke and darkness they are like the flowers

we have seen growing
through the dust of eroded slopes,
their slowly opening faces turned toward the mountain.

Carved in devotion, their eyes
have softened through age and their mouths
curve through delight of the carver's hand.

If only our own faces
would allow the invisible carver's hand
to bring the deep grain of love to the surface.

If only we knew
as the carver knew, how the flaws
in the wood led his searching chisel to the very core,

we would smile too
and not need faces immobilized
by fear and the weight of things undone.

When we fight with our failings, we ignore
the entrance to the shrine itself and wrestle
with the guardian, fierce figure on the side of good.

And as we fight
our eyes are hooded with grief
and our mouths are dry with pain.

If only we could give ourselves
to the blows of the carver's hands,
the lines in our faces would be the trace lines of rivers

feeding the sea
where voices meet, praising the features
of the mountain and the cloud and the sky.

Our faces would fall away
until we, growing younger toward death
every day, would gather all our flaws in celebration

to merge with them perfectly,
impossibly, wedded to our essence,
full of silence from the carver's hands.

THE FACES AT BRAGA   *Placed firmly in my memory, a recollected collective experience of entering a then-remote monastery high in the Himalayas… In the darkness of the vestibule, waiting for one of our number to find the one flashlight we knew we had somewhere between us, I bumped into the carved temple guardian, or Vajrapani, with the same shock we might have bumping into a live person in the dark. The invitation in that encounter was to a robust living vulnerability, a willingness to embrace all difficulties and personal flaws as did the astonishingly carved, compassionate faces we found inside. Looking up at the carved figures, arrayed above us in the candlelight, I felt a revelatory wave of shock and a seeming recognition pass through us all. 'The Faces at Braga' was written to uncover the essence of that experience.*

The Sea in You

When I wake under the moon, I do not know
who I have become unless I move closer to you,
obeying the give and take of the earth as it breathes
the slender length of your body, so that in breathing
with the tide that breathes in you, and moving
with you as you come and go, and following you,
half in light and half in dark, I feel the first firm edge
of my floating palm touch and then trace the pale
light of your shoulder, to the faint moonlit shadow
of your smooth cheek, and drawing my finger through
the pearl water of your skin, I sense the breath
on your lips touch and then warm, the finest, furthest,
most unknown edge of my sense of self,
so that I come to you under the moon as if I had
swum under the deepest arch of the ocean,
to find you living where no one could possibly live,
and to feel you breathing where no one could possibly
breathe, and I touch your skin as I would
touch a pale whispering spirit of the tides, that my arms
try to hold with the wrong kind of strength and my
lips try to speak with the wrong kind of love and I follow
you through the ocean night listening for your breath
in my helpless calling to love you as I should, and I lie
next to you in my sleep as I would next to the sea,
overwhelmed by the rest that arrives in me and by
the weight that is taken from me and what, by morning,
is left on the shore of my waking joy.

Love in the Night

Sometimes when you lie close to me,
your body is so still in my arms
I find myself half in love with your
barely breathing form and half in love
with the unspeaking silent source
from which you come. I find myself
touching your lips with mine
to feel their warmth and bowing my head
to hear your breath, and stilling myself
to listen far inside you for the gentle rise
and fall of the tide that tells me
you are still free to come and go in life,
so that I take your hand in mine to sense
your pulse and touch your hair
and stroke your cheek and move my lips
to yours to feel the warmth emerging
from your inward self and to
see we are still here and still pledged
to breathe this world together.

All night like this I find myself asleep
and awake, turned toward the moon
and then turned toward you, your warmth
inviting me to bring you close
and leave you alone, all night I find myself
unable to choose between the love
I feel for you through closeness
and the grief of having to let you go
through distance, so that it seems
I can only breathe fully in the dark

by taking you in and giving you away
in your quiet rhythm of appearance
and disappearance, letting you return
in your breathing and not breathing,
or your half-sighed phrases spoken
to the dark, whispered from the dream
in which you live, so that I lie
between sleeping and waking,
seeing you are here and dreaming you are gone,
wanting to hold you and wanting to let you go,

living far inside you as you breathe close to me,
and living far beyond you, as I wait through
the hours of the night for you to wake
and find me again, the light in your eyes
half-dreaming on the pillow
looking back at me, and seeing me at last,

not knowing how far I have travelled,
through what distance I have come to find you,
where I have been, or what I have seen,
how far or how near; not knowing how
I have gained and lost you a hundred times
between darkness and dawn.

LOVE IN THE NIGHT *Falling in love is experienced physically like a real 'falling', the disorienting sense of ground giving way toward the mysterious tidal embrace of the other, or more disturbingly, falling toward a part of our self we had never quite understood, toward a form of happiness we often feel we do not deserve, and to a depth we did not feel we could venture to breathe in, 'as if swimming under the deepest arch of the ocean.' There is also a strange, tidal coming and going of edges and boundaries, influenced by everything it seems but our own will.*

In love we subvert the everyday structures of the life we had built so carefully and raze them to foundations on which a new, shared life can be built again. Unrequited love has its own form of fearful falling, but falling into a full felt and reciprocated love we face the most difficult, most revealing and most beautiful questions of all: are we large enough and generous enough and present enough; are we deserving enough, and ready enough to hold the joy, the future grief, and the overwhelming sense of privileged blessing that lies in that embrace?

To Break a Promise

Make a place of prayer, no fuss now,
just lean into the white brilliance
and say what you needed to say
all along, nothing too much, words
as simple and as yours and as heard
as the bird song above your head
or the river running gently beside you.

Let your words join one to another
the way stone nestles on stone,
the way water just leaves
and goes to the sea,
the way your promise
breathes and belongs
with every other promise
the world has ever made.

Now, let them go on,
leave your words
to carry their own life
without you, let the promise
go with the river.

Stand up now. Have faith. Walk away.

TO BREAK A PROMISE *Everywhere in our religious and artistic traditions, we are told how to make and hold to promises, and yet there is almost nothing in our literature to help us in the necessary art of breaking outworn, misguided, or out-of-season bonds that are now obscuring the underlying vow that led us to the commitment in the first place. Breaking promises is something most human beings have to do often, in order to remain true to the deeper underlying current of their lives and, just as often, the lives of those to whom they made the promise: but it is not something we often do well. This poem was written for a letting go that happened in the right kind of way, walking away from a promise that was no longer a promise for the future but an imprisoning bond to an abstract past.*

This poem could also live under the alternative title of 'To Make a Promise', a radical human act that calls for the same kind of leaning into the interior 'white brilliance' of truth as any promise we may have made. In the making of a necessary promise or in the necessary breaking of a promise, when we do find the core living words that speak for where we need to go or how we need to be, the words themselves have their own power, their own sweet way to take us on; and a need to be left alone to have their own life as a promise themselves, as an invitational mystery, an emblem of our courage, something thereafter to be lived up to and into.

Faith

I want to write about faith,
    about the way the moon rises
        over cold snow, night after night,

faithful even as it fades from fullness,
    slowly becoming that last curving and impossible
        sliver of light before the final darkness.

But I have no faith myself
    I refuse it even the smallest entry.

Let this then, my small poem,
    like a new moon, slender and barely open,
        be the first prayer that opens me to faith.

FAITH *'Faith' was written in a wondering moment, at the very beginning of my risking myself as 'a poet' in the world, in the daylight basement room of a friend's house; a wonder focused on the many disappearances which seemed to accompany my having stepped out along the uncharted vocational path as a full-time poet, whatever that mysterious term might mean. It was a way of reminding myself of the necessity for the 'radical simplifications' that only from the outside look like bravery. Most importantly, of the necessity for a friendship with the unknown that lay before me, held mythologically in both the interior darkness of our bodies and the body of the night sky by the way the moon first fades and then disappears completely for three days and nights of every month of every year of every life on this planet.*

The Well of Grief

Those who will not slip beneath
    the still surface on the well of grief,

turning down through its black water,
    to the place we cannot breathe,

will never know the source from which we drink,
    the secret water cold and clear,

nor find in the darkness glimmering,
    the small round coins,
        thrown by those who wished for something else.

THE WELL OF GRIEF *As a very serious young poet with a destination in mind, I decided to write a long and in-depth narrative poem on grief. There was an immediate physical sense of dropping down, dropping down through the body, dropping down through the gravitational pull of each line on the page, as if leaning down ever further to drink from a deeper source. Within six lines I caught a glimmer on the bottom of that well and despite my first attempts to ignore it, and to get back to my long epic, I knew the poem was over.*

All round the world, in all cultures we throw coins into wells to make a wish – this was the first time that I understood so physically that the wish is defensive and propitious. The essence of the wish is that we will be absolved from having to descend into the source ourselves. The coins take all kinds of forms, some of us have thrown marriages, friendships, hopes and dreams and, most of all, our necessary and robust vulnerabilities down there in the hope that the greater and more golden the sacrifice, the more it will absolve us from having to go down to that source – and a true physical and foundational understanding of the grief we carry with us. The Well of Grief.

Mameen

Be infinitesimal under that sky, a creature
even the sailing hawk misses, a wraith
among the rocks where the mist parts slowly.

Recall the way mere mortals are overwhelmed
by circumstance, how great reputations
dissolve with infirmity and how you,
in particular, stand a hairsbreadth from losing
everyone you hold dear.

Then, look back down the path to the north,
the way you came, as if seeing
your entire past and then south
over the hazy blue coast as if present
to a broad future.

Recall the way you are all possibilities
you can see and how you live best
as an appreciator of horizons
whether you reach them or not.

Admit, that once you have got up
from your chair and opened the door,
once you have walked out into the clean air
toward that edge and taken the path up high
beyond the ordinary, you have become

the privileged and the pilgrim,
the one who will tell the story
and the one, coming back

from the mountain
who helped to make it.

MAMEEN   *In 'Deepest Connemara' in Ireland the veil seems
very thin between this world and the next, between those
still living and those who have gone before us. The ancient
conversation between the mountains and the sea and the passing
sky magnifies one of the most extraordinary capabilities of
human beings: to hold many contexts and many conversations
and even many lives, lived and unlived together in one central
imagination. This poem is dedicated to John O'Donohue, who
first took me up to Mameen, as one who would introduce one
very good friend to another very good friend. John was one
who held enormous, wide-ranging, multi-layered contexts and
who still lives on as a companion to my imagination and my
everyday speech as much as he did when he could cast a shadow
and talk and walk and dream with me along the endless ridge
lines and shorelines between mountain and sea.*

What to Remember when Waking

In that first
hardly noticed
moment
in which you wake,
coming back
to this life
from the other
more secret,
moveable
and frighteningly
honest
world
where everything
began,
there is a small
opening
into the day
that closes
the moment
you begin
your plans.

What you can plan
is too small
for you to live.

What you can live
wholeheartedly
will make plans

enough for the vitality
hidden in your sleep.

To become human
is to become visible
while carrying
what is hidden
as a gift to others.

To remember
the other world
in this world
is to live in your
true inheritance.

You are not
a troubled guest
on this earth,
you are not
an accident
amidst other accidents,
you were invited
from another and greater
night than the one
from which
you have just emerged.

Now, looking through
the slanting light
of the morning window
toward the mountain presence
of everything that can be,
what urgency
calls you
to your one love?

What shape
waits in the seed of you
to grow and spread
its branches
against a future sky?

Is it waiting
in the fertile sea?
In the trees
beyond the house?
In the life
you can imagine
for yourself?

In the open
and lovely
white page
on the waiting desk?

WHAT TO REMEMBER WHEN WAKING *looks at the crucial moment of re-entry into the physical world that astonishingly each of us experiences every morning of our waking. There is a whole cargo of revelation flowing out of that radically re-imagined state we call sleep, ready to inform the newly woken on even the most average workaday morning. Deep sleep is not only a revitalization of the body but a revolution of our sense of self and our understanding of the particular decisive threshold on which we now stand. Waking up into even the most ordinary day is a discipline, a test of our ability to hold the interior world, where we have just been re-imagined and revolutionized, with the moving, tidal, seasonal, not to be controlled, physical world we are just about enter. What to Remember when Waking.*

Coleman's Bed

Make a nesting now, a place to which
the birds can come, think of Kevin's
prayerful palm holding the blackbird's egg
and be the one, looking out from this place
who warms interior forms into light.
Feel the way the cliff at your back
gives shelter to your outward view
and then bring in from those horizons
all discordant elements that seek a home.

Be taught now, among the trees and rocks,
how the discarded is woven into shelter,
learn the way things hidden and unspoken
slowly proclaim their voice in the world.
Find that far inward symmetry
to all outward appearances, apprentice
yourself to yourself, begin to welcome back
all you sent away, be a new annunciation,
make yourself a door through which
to be hospitable, even to the stranger in you.

See with every turning day,
how each season wants to make a child
of you again, wants you to become
a seeker after rainfall and birdsong,
watch now, how it weathers you to a testing
in the tried and true, tells you
with each falling leaf, to leave and slip away,
even from that branch that held you,

to go when you need to, to be courageous,
to be like that last word you'd want to say
before you leave the world.

Above all, be alone with it all,
a hiving off, a corner of silence
amidst the noise, refuse to talk,
even to yourself, and stay in this place
until the current of the story
is strong enough to float you out.

Ghost then, to where others
in this place have come before,
under the hazel, by the ruined chapel,
below the cave where Coleman slept,
become the source that makes
the river flow, and then the sea
beyond. Live in this place
as you were meant to, and then,
surprised by your abilities,
become the ancestor of it all,
the quiet, robust and blessed Saint
that your future happiness
will always remember.

COLEMAN'S BED *I was thirteen consecutive years visiting Saint Coleman's retreat in the Burren mountains of North Clare before I felt able to write this piece for this very, very invitational place: a cave and a ruined chapel nestled above the hazel wood, beside a fresh spring and sheltered by a limestone cliff. Coleman was a powerful agent of political and societal change, who helped not only to transform Irish society but post-Roman Europe, sending monks out from the Irish Church to form islands of cultural, contemplative and agricultural sanity into the most remote parts of a violent and beleaguered continent. The place and the life remembered are exemplary. This poem is written to represent the series of ever deeper questions that the place makes to each pilgrim visitor and looks at the way we settle best into a place in the same way we settle into our own bodies, as a series of invitations. The rested journey into the breath and the body we inhabit is the same pilgrimage we make into the outer landscape and body of the world. There is always an unspoken question behind every pilgrimage, an unspoken question I found answered in the lovely and surprising revelation that came to me at the end of the poem.*

Seven Streams

Come down drenched, at the end of May,
with the cold rain so far into your bones
that nothing will warm you except your
own walking, and let the sun come out
at day's end by Slievenaglusha
with the rainbows doubling over Mulloch Mor
and see your clothes steaming in the bright air.

Be a provenance of something gathered,
a summation of previous intuitions,
let your vulnerabilities walking
on the cracked sliding limestone
be this time, not a weakness, but a faculty
for understanding what's about to happen.

Stand above the Seven Streams
letting the deep-down current surface
around you, then branch and branch
as they do, back into the mountain
and as if you were able for that flow,
say the few necessary words
and walk on, broader and cleansed
for having imagined.

SEVEN STREAMS *The Seven Streams are a geographical and mythological anomaly in a remote part of the Burren mountains of North Clare; an ancient, difficult to find, place of sanctity and healing. The water is pure, as is the air. Cupping our hands to drink, we feel a far inward symmetry to all this outer, thirst-quenching clarity emanating from the limestone rock. The water appears from beneath a limestone escarpment, creates a clear, wide pool, then meanders through a short, shallow valley before disappearing, like our own lives, to appear again, seemingly defying the laws of physics by reappearing as seven separate flows beneath the cliff below. It is always a place that points to what is essential, what must be uncovered, and what must be let rest, to go its own way. The Seven Streams.*

The House of Belonging

I awoke
this morning
in the gold light
turning this way
and that

thinking for
a moment
it was one
day
like any other.

But
the veil had gone
from my
darkened heart
and
I thought

it must have been the quiet
candlelight
that filled my room,

it must have been
the first
easy rhythm
with which I breathed
myself to sleep,

it must have been
the prayer I said
speaking to the otherness
of the night.

And
I thought
this is the good day
you could
meet your love,

this is the grey day
someone close
to you could die.

This is the day
you realize
how easily the thread
is broken
between this world
and the next

and I found myself
sitting up
in the quiet pathway
of light,

the tawny
close-grained cedar
burning round

me like fire
and all the angels
of this housely
heaven ascending
through the first
roof of light
the sun had made.

This is the bright home
in which I live,
this is where
I ask
my friends
to come,
this is where I want
to love all the things
it has taken me so long
to learn to love.

This is the temple
of my adult aloneness
and I belong
to that aloneness
as I belong to my life.

There is no house
like the house of belonging.

THE HOUSE OF BELONGING   *One of the interesting dynamics of coming to ground, of suddenly having a sense of a real home and foundation again, is that it actually restores our relationship with the far, beckoning horizon of our life and gives us a proper sense of the future. This piece was begun to mark one of those powerful threshold experiences over which we seem to have no powers of personal manipulation. 'The House of Belonging' was written after waking up into a strong, almost tidal sense of new arrival in my life, a literal morning waking in a very old house that was very new to me, the weather of difficulty and heartache under which I had journeyed to get there swept away in the morning light, and the sudden realization that I was in a new place and in a new conversation with the future.*

The Opening of Eyes

That day I saw beneath dark clouds
the passing light over the water
and I heard the voice of the world speak out,
I knew then, as I had before
life is no passing memory of what has been
nor the remaining pages in a great book
waiting to be read.

It is the opening of eyes long closed.
It is the vision of far off things
seen for the silence they hold.
It is the heart after years
of secret conversing
speaking out loud in the clear air.

It is Moses in the desert
fallen to his knees before the lit bush.
It is the man throwing away his shoes
as if to enter heaven
and finding himself astonished,
opened at last,
fallen in love with solid ground.

THE OPENING OF EYES *Caught by a ray of light,*
something dramatically outlined in the outer world can find
an equivalent deep-down symmetry inside us, as we look on,
illuminating an as yet un-encountered part of ourselves, just
beginning to make itself known, bringing inner and outer
horizons together in one moment. This is the experience I
had years ago, living in the mountains of Snowdonia, when I
climbed the ridge behind my caravan to solve a difficult outer
dilemma and reaching the top, looked over the sea toward
Ireland. 'The Opening of Eyes', looks at the way that at any
crucial moment in our life, there is never a choice between left or
right, this way or that, it is always about taking a way forward
that holds the two creatively together. In the midst of this
understanding, the poem captures my new and flooding sense of
something just about to be understood.

Second Sight

Sometimes, you need the ocean light,
and colours you've never seen before
painted through an evening sky.

Sometimes you need your God
to be a simple invitation,
not a telling word of wisdom.

Sometimes you need only the first shyness
that comes from being shown things
far beyond your understanding,

so that you can fly and become free
by being still and by being still here.

And then there are times you need to be
brought to ground by touch
and touch alone.

To know those arms around you
and to make your home in the world.
just by being wanted.

To see those eyes looking back at you,
as eyes should see you at last,

seeing you, as you always wanted to be seen,
seeing you, as you yourself
had always wanted to see the world.

SECOND SIGHT   *The sense of the loved one seeing themselves through the intensity with which you are seeing them – and the reciprocation of that seeing – is the essence of the mutual, loving gaze. It is not confined to the merely human. Looking intensely at a landscape or the ocean, the give and take of the shoreline where the two meet, we fall in love, and perhaps equally, even find ourselves with a sense of being loved by the tidal essence of the world that we inhabit.*

The Truelove

There is a faith in loving fiercely
the one who is rightfully yours,
especially if you have
waited years and especially
if part of you never believed
you could deserve this
loved and beckoning hand
held out to you this way.

I am thinking of faith now
and the testaments of loneliness
and what we feel we are
worthy of in this world.

Years ago, in the Hebrides
I remember an old man
who walked every morning
on the grey stones
to the shore of the baying seals,

who would press his hat
to his chest in the blustering
salt wind and say his prayer
to the turbulent Jesus
hidden in the water,

and I think of the story
of the storm and everyone
waking and seeing
the distant

yet familiar figure
far across the water
calling to them,

and how we are all
preparing for that
abrupt waking,
and that calling,
and that moment
we have to say yes,
except it will
not come so grandly,
so Biblically,
but more subtly
and intimately in the face
of the one you know
you have to love,

so that when we finally
step out of the boat
toward them, we find
everything holds us
and everything confirms
our courage, and if you wanted
to drown you could,
but you don't
because finally
after all the struggle
and all the years,
you don't want to any more,

you've simply had enough
of drowning
and you want to live and you
want to love and you will
walk across any territory
and any darkness,
however fluid and however
dangerous, to take the
one hand you know
belongs in yours.

THE TRUELOVE *The beautiful surprise of arrival, having found the way opening before you into an overwhelming but marvelous invitation: across water, across new country, through another person's eyes, seeing and being seen inside and outside. A surface that before seemed hardly able to bear our weight, now a foundation.*

This poem has been recited now at hundreds of weddings around the world, most particularly for those for whom being visible in relationship, and most especially in marriage, was a courageous act in itself. It is more than a solace to the poet writing in a quiet, hermetic privacy, to have a few words become so beautifully and publicly communal.

Santiago

The road seen, then not seen, the hillside hiding
then revealing the way you should take, the road
dropping away from you as if leaving you to walk
on thin air, then catching you, holding you up,
when you thought you would fall, and the way
forward always in the end the way that you followed,
the way that carried you into your future, that brought
you to this place, no matter that it sometimes took
your promise from you, no matter that it had to break
your heart along the way: the sense of having walked
from far inside yourself out into the revelation,
to have risked yourself for something that seemed
to stand both inside you and far beyond you,
that called you back in the end to the only road
you could follow, walking as you did, in your rags
of love and speaking in the voice that by night
became a prayer for safe arrival, so that one day
you realized that what you wanted had already
happened, and long ago and in the dwelling place
in which you had lived in before you began,
and that every step along the way, you had carried
the heart and the mind and the promise
that first set you off and then drew you on
and that, you were more marvelous in your
simple wish to find a way than the gilded roofs
of any destination you could reach:
as if, all along, you had thought the end point
might be a city with golden domes, and cheering
crowds, and turning the corner at what you thought

was the end of the road, you found just a simple
reflection, and a clear revelation beneath the face
looking back and beneath it another invitation,
all in one glimpse: like a person or a place
you had sought forever, like a broad field of freedom
that beckoned you beyond; like another life,
and the road still stretching on.

SANTIAGO   'You were more marvelous in your simple wish to find a way': a line that might perhaps just encapsulate the ultimate form of faith: faith in the way we are made for the conversation; for the way we have taken, and that we look back upon, strangely only to see the path we took forward. The simple wish to find a way we can call our own through all the trials and tribulations and beautiful humiliations, and the radical act of daring to be happy along that way as we go.

The road in the end taking the path the sun
had taken, into the western sea, and the moon
rising behind you, as you stood where ground
turned to ocean: no way to your future now
except the way your shadow could take, walking
before you across water, going where shadows go,
no way to make sense of a world that wouldn't
let you pass, except to call an end to the way
you had come, to take out each frayed letter
you had brought and light their illumined corners;
and to read them as they drifted on the late
western light: to empty your bags; to sort this
and to leave that; to promise what you needed to
promise all along, and to abandon the shoes
that brought you here right at the water's edge,
not because you had given up but because now
you would find a different way to tread,
and because, through it all, part of you would
still walk on, no matter how, over the waves.

FINISTERRE *My Irish niece (by ancient right of fosterage),*
Marlene McCormack, completed her studies in Irish drama
and set off into the world, not to teach drama, but become a
dramatist herself, a vocational path for which one does not
receive much earthly corroboration in this life. Being good to
herself, she decided to begin this uncharted vocational path by
walking another parallel pilgrim path, the Camino de Santiago
de Compostela.

Driving in her company through a rainy night in Seattle
just after her completion of this 500-mile odyssey across
northern Spain, I asked her what the most powerful and
transformative moment had been on the entire trail. She replied
that it had been at the very end, after the city of Santiago,
reaching the wild edges of the Atlantic shore, at a place aptly
named Finisterre, The Ends of the Earth, and then she
described it in some detail. Fighting against the temptation to
pull over to the side of the road and start writing immediately, I
finished the poem at home at about two in the morning while
everyone was a-bed, including Marlene. I gave her the piece to
read at breakfast. Finisterre: The Ends of the Earth.

Everything is Waiting for You
(After Derek Mahon)

Your great mistake is to act the drama
as if you were alone. As if life
were a progressive and cunning crime
with no witness to the tiny hidden
transgressions. To feel abandoned is to deny
the intimacy of your surroundings. Surely,
even you, at times, have felt the grand array;
the swelling presence, and the chorus, crowding
out your solo voice. You must note
the way the soap dish enables you,
or the window latch grants you freedom.
Alertness is the hidden discipline of familiarity.
The stairs are your mentor of things
to come, the doors have always been there
to frighten you and invite you,
and the tiny speaker in the phone
is your dream-ladder to divinity.

Put down the weight of your aloneness and ease
into the conversation. The kettle is singing
even as it pours you a drink, the cooking pots
have left their arrogant aloofness and
seen the good in you at last. All the birds
and creatures of the world are unutterably
themselves. Everything is waiting for you.

EVERYTHING IS WAITING FOR YOU *The ancient intuition, corroborated only in our more profound states of attention and intentionality, of identity – not as a fixed or nameable commodity but more like a meeting, a call-and-answer song, a continual surprise. This surprising identity is one with equally surprising allies in the world, like the colour blue or a sudden doorway, or even a soap dish or a window latch – an identity that is enriched and deepened the more we pay attention to what is other than ourselves. Everything is Waiting for You.*

The Bell and the Blackbird

The sound
of a bell
still reverberating,

or a blackbird
calling
from a corner
of a field
asking you to wake
into this life
or inviting you
deeper
to one that waits,

either way
takes courage,
either way wants you
to be nothing
but that self that
is no self at all,
wants you to walk
to the place
where you find
you already know
how to give
every last thing
away.

The approach
that is also
the meeting
itself,
without any
meeting
at all.

That radiance
you have always
carried with you
as you walk
both alone
and completely
accompanied
in friendship
by every corner
of the world
crying
'Alleluia'.

Blessing for the Morning Light

The blessing of the morning light to you,
may it find you even in your invisible
appearances, may you be seen to have risen
from some other place you know and have known
in the darkness and that carries all you need.
May you see what is hidden in you as a place
of hospitality and shadowed shelter,
may what is hidden in you become your gift
to give, may you hold that shadow to the light
and the silence of that shelter to the word
of the light, may you join all of your previous
disappearances with this new appearance,
this new morning, this being seen again,
new and newly alive.

BLESSING FOR THE MORNING LIGHT *Perhaps there is nothing we take more for granted than the everyday light delineating our world and the faces of our loved ones, though sometimes we are tempted to appreciate only its ability to outline all our grounds for complaint. A reminder and a blessing, therefore, for those most basic ways; and at the same time those most astounding physical and beyond-physical ways that light forms our self-understandings and our perceptions of this world. Blessing for the Light.*

A Seeming Stillness

We love the movement in a seeming stillness,
the breath in the body of the loved one sleeping,
the highest leaves in the silent wood,
a great migration in the sky above:
the waters of the earth, the blood in the body,
the first, soft, stir in the silence beneath a strident
voice, the internal hands of our mind,
always searching for touch, thoughts seeking other
thoughts, seeking other minds, the great arrival
of form through all our hidden themes.

And this breath, in this body, able,
just for a moment to give and to take,
to ask and be told, to find and be found,
to bless and be blessed, to hold and be held.

We are all a sun-lit moment come from
a long darkness, what moves us always
comes from what is hidden, what seems
to be said so suddenly has lived
in the body for a long, long time.

Our life like a breath, then, a give
and a take, a bridge, a central movement,
between singing a separate self
and learning to be selfless.

Breathe then, as if breathing for the first time,
as if remembering with what difficulty
you came into the world, what strength it took
to make that first impossible in-breath,
into a cry to be heard by the world.

Your essence has always been that first vulnerability
of being found, of being heard and of being seen,
and from the very beginning
the one who has always needed,
and been given, so much invisible help.

This is how you were when you first came
into the world, this is how you were
when you took your first breath in that world,
this is how you are now,
all unawares, in your new body and your new life,
this is the raw vulnerability of your every day,
and this is how you will want to be,
and be remembered, when you leave the world.

A SEEMING STILLNESS *One very still summer morning in Granada, Spain, waiting outside the coffee shop, Barista Durán – a place that may serve not only the very best coffee in Spain but also acts as my temporary morning writing studio – I found myself looking over the balustrade of the river Darro at a spreading tree whose highest leaves were being imperceptibly disturbed by the gentle breeze descending from the Sierra Nevada, like a river itself from mountains, and asking myself why, as human beings, we always find movement out of a seeming stillness so beautiful. Sitting to write inside the café, the image of a breathing loved one amidst the seeming stillness of sleep arrived first and the poem went on from there. A very memorable morning that concluded almost a year later in the same coffee shop, with lines entering a territory of sheer, raw, physical undoing, that surprised me, belying the poem's subtle beginnings.*

Fintan

The pool near Slane, where hazel brushes the gleam
of water and the just ripe nut touches and un-touches
the still cold darkness of a shaded stream, the wet
encircled shell a meniscus of light for the rising mouth
of a silvered salmon, scale and sleek. The moon,
the wait, the strike, the plash of dawn-lit water,
whoever ate this fish that fed on the tree of life,
whoever caught and cooked and then consumed
the flesh of the messenger-god, would make no king,
would uncover no gold to hoard against the coming
awe, would become mortal-wise through words
enfleshed with the nut of truth, would become equal
to the task of living and dying, a man acknowledged,
as one who *could* now speak for others, who *would* now
speak for others, greatest of poets in a land of poets.

is what we almost always are: close to happiness, close to one another, close to leaving, close to tears, close to God, close to losing faith, close to being done, close to saying something, or sometimes tantalizingly close to success, and even, with the greatest sense of satisfaction, close to giving the whole thing up.

Our human essence lies not in arrival, but in being almost there: we are creatures who are on our way, our journey a series of impending anticipated arrivals. We live by unconsciously measuring the inverse distances of our proximity: an intimacy calibrated by the vulnerability we feel in giving up our sense of separation.

To go beyond our normal identities and become closer than close is to lose our sense of self in temporary joy: a form of arrival that only opens us to deeper forms of intimacy that blur our fixed, controlling, surface identity.

To consciously become close is a courageous form of unilateral disarmament, a chancing of our arm and our love, a willingness to hazard our affections and an unconscious declaration that we might be equal to the inevitable loss that the vulnerability of being close will bring.

Human beings do not find their essence through fulfillment or eventual arrival but by staying close to the way they like to travel, to the way they hold the conversation between the ground on which they stand and the horizon to which they go. We are in effect, always close; always close to the ultimate secret: that we are more real in our simple wish to find a way than any destination we could reach: the step between not understanding that and understanding that, is as close as we get to happiness.

is a way of staying alive. Hiding is a way of holding
ourselves until we are ready to come into the light.
Hiding is one of the brilliant and virtuoso practices of
almost every part of the natural world: the protective
quiet of an icy northern landscape, the held bud of a
future summer rose, the snow-bound internal pulse of
the hibernating bear. Hiding is underestimated. We
are hidden by life in our mother's womb until we grow
and ready ourselves for our first appearance in the
lighted world; to appear too early in that world is to
find ourselves with the immediate necessity for outside
intensive care.

Hiding done properly is the internal faithful
promise for a proper future emergence, as embryos, as
children or even as emerging adults in retreat from the
names that have caught us and imprisoned us, often in
ways where we have been too easily seen and too easily
named. We live in a time of the dissected soul, the
immediate disclosure; our thoughts, imaginings and
longings exposed to the light too much, too early and
too often, our best qualities squeezed too soon into a
world already awash with ideas that oppress our sense
of self and our sense of others. What is real is almost
always, to begin with, hidden and does not want to be
understood by the part of our mind that mistakenly
thinks it knows what is happening. What is precious
inside us does not care to be known by the mind in ways
that diminish its presence.

Hiding is an act of freedom from the misunder-
standing of others, especially in the enclosing world

of oppressive secret government and private entities, attempting to name us, to anticipate us, to leave us with no place to hide and grow in ways unmanaged by a creeping necessity for absolute naming, absolute tracking and absolute control. Hiding is a bid for independence, from others, from mistaken ideas we have about ourselves, from an oppressive and mistaken wish to keep us completely safe, completely ministered to, and therefore completely managed. Hiding is creative, necessary and beautifully subversive of outside interference and control. Hiding leaves life to itself, to become more of itself. Hiding is the radical independence necessary for our emergence into the light of a proper human future.

HIDING   *I once found a fugitive little row boat hiding under branches, as if waiting for me to leap in and row it away, on the River Cong in County Mayo by the ruins of the old monastery that clings to its banks. It seemed to me to represent that deeply felt human need to creatively and subversively disappear; to turn away from the over-lighted human world and not be found so that we can actually catch up with ourselves and reappear in the world again more as we intuit we can be, possibly re-imagined, reinvigorated, regrown and rested; un-confined by the names we have accrued in the overly managed, human social worlds we are often forced to inhabit.*

To my mind, one of the great necessary inner disciplines is the ability to stay close to what is still hidden and unannounced in us, the interior 'deep but dazzling darkness' out of which any new and worthwhile future will be announced.

takes us in when we have nowhere else to go; when we feel the heart cannot break anymore, when our world or our loved ones disappear, when we feel we cannot be loved or do not deserve to be loved, when our God disappoints, or when our body is carrying profound pain in a way that does not seem to go away.

Despair is a haven with its own temporary form of beauty and of self-compassion, it is the invitation we accept when we want to remove ourselves from hurt.

Despair is a last protection. To disappear through despair, is to seek a temporary but necessary illusion, a place where we hope nothing can ever find us in the same way again.

Despair is a necessary and seasonal state of repair, a temporary healing absence, an internal physiological and psychological winter when our previous forms of participation in the world take a rest; it is a loss of horizon, it is the place we go to when we do not want to be found in the same way anymore. We give up hope when certain particular wishes are no longer able to come true and despair is the time in which we both endure and heal, even when we have not yet found the new form of hope.

Despair is strangely, the last bastion of hope; the wish being, that if we cannot be found in the old way, we cannot ever be touched or hurt in that way again. Despair is the sweet but illusory abstraction of leaving the body while still inhabiting it, so we can stop the body from feeling anymore. Despair is the place we go to when we no longer want to make a home in the world and where we feel, with a beautifully cruel form of satisfaction, that we may never have deserved that home in the first place. Despair, strangely, has its own sense of achievement, and despair, even more strangely, needs despair to keep it alive.

Despair turns to depression and abstraction when we try to make it stay beyond its appointed season and start to shape our identity around its frozen disappointments. But despair can only stay beyond its appointed time through the forced artificiality of created distance, by abstracting ourselves from bodily feeling, by trapping ourselves in the disappointed mind, by convincing ourselves that the seasons have stopped and can never turn again and, perhaps most simply and importantly, by refusing to let the body breathe by itself, fully and deeply. Despair is kept alive by freezing our sense of time and the rhythms of time; when we no longer feel imprisoned by time, and when the season is allowed to turn, despair cannot survive.

To keep despair alive, we have to abstract and immobilize our bodies, our faculties of hearing, touch and smell, and keep the surrounding springtime of the world at a distance. Despair needs a certain tending, a reinforcing, and isolation, but the body left to itself will breathe, the ears will hear the first birdsong of morning or catch the leaves being touched by the wind in the trees, and the wind will blow away even the grayest cloud; will move even the most immovable season; the heart will continue to beat and the world, we realize, will never stop or go away.

The antidote to despair is not to be found in the brave attempt to cheer ourselves up with happy abstracts, but in paying a profound and courageous attention to the body and the breath, independent of our imprisoning thoughts and stories – even, strangely, in paying attention to despair itself, and the way we hold it, and which we realize, was never ours to own and to hold in the first place. To see and experience despair fully in our body is to begin to see it as a necessary, seasonal visitation, and the first step in letting it have its own life, neither holding it nor moving it on before its time.

We take the first steps out of despair by taking on its full weight and coming fully to ground in our wish not to be here. We let our bodies and we let our world breathe again. In that place, strangely, despair cannot do anything but change into something else, into some other season, as it was meant to do, from the beginning. Despair is a difficult, beautiful necessity, a binding understanding between human beings caught in a fierce and difficult world where half of our experience is mediated by loss, but it is a season, a waveform passing through the body, not a prison surrounding us. A season left to itself will always move, however slowly, under its own patience, power and volition.

Refusing to despair about despair itself, we can let despair have its own natural life and take a first step onto the foundational ground of human compassion, the ability to see and understand and touch and even speak, the heartfelt grief of another.

DESPAIR *I am not a despairing person, and certainly, in the buoyancy of my present days I feel very, very far from that apparent state of giving in and giving up, but it was not too many years ago, telephone pressed against my ear, in the late night anonymity of a hotel room, hearing of the sudden loss of a close friend, that I felt the quiet hand of despair rest on my shoulder as she turned me resolutely to look her full in the face. In that giving over I felt for just a very few moments as if I had on my tongue, the unadulterated and unwanted pure malt taste of devastation and despair. It was a kind of fainting, and indeed I found myself a moment later, kneeling against the bed. I was astonished at the physical nature of the prostration, as if the body needed to give up holding its own weight, as if it simply couldn't hold its own weight anymore, as if it demanded to fall against something other than its own self; the way the forehead, that outer representation of the way we lead ourselves in thought, resting against the covers, simply did not want to be the one leading my thinking or knowing anymore.*

I was even more astonished to feel in that depth, how much of a different form of shelter and care waits for us beneath the outer forms of giving up, how that hand on the shoulder becomes a hand around the shoulder, and how a strange and marvelous mercy becomes available to us only in our sheer vulnerability, as if in stopping a certain way of holding the world I could allow myself to be held myself, in a different way. Despair, it seems, asks for its own difficult form of faith, extends its hand in a form of friendship we do not at first comprehend. It is as if as human beings, no matter its outward form, we find it impossible to live in the world without some sense of home; that even in despair we are able to find another beautiful form of shelter, a home at the core when all outer homes seem to have been stolen away.

is a mirror to presence and a testament to forgiveness. Friendship not only helps us see ourselves through another's eyes, but can be sustained over the years only with someone who has repeatedly forgiven us for our trespasses as we must find it in ourselves to forgive them in turn. A friend knows our difficulties and shadows and remains in sight, a companion to our vulnerabilities more than our triumphs, when we are under the strange illusion we do not need them. An undercurrent of real friendship is a blessing exactly because its elemental form is rediscovered again and again through understanding and mercy. All friendships of any length are based on a continued, mutual forgiveness. Without tolerance and mercy all friendships die.

Friendship is the great hidden transmuter of all relationship: it can transform a troubled marriage, make honorable a professional rivalry, make sense of heartbreak and unrequited love and become the newly discovered ground for a mature parent–child relationship.

The dynamic of friendship is almost always under-estimated as a constant force in human life: a diminish-ing circle of friends is the first terrible diagnostic of a life in deep trouble: of overwork, of too much emphasis on a professional identity, of forgetting who will be there when our armored personalities run into the inevitable natural disasters and vulnerabilities found in even the most average existence.

Through the eyes of a friend we especially learn to remain at least a little interesting to others. When we flatten our personalities and lose our curiosity in the life of the world or of another, friendship loses spirit and animation; boredom is the second great killer of friendship. Through the natural surprises of a relationship held through the passage of years we recognize the greater surprising circles of which we are a part and the faithfulness that sustains a wider sense of revelation, independent of human relationship: to learn to be friends with the earth and the sky, with the horizon and with the seasons, even with the disappearances of winter, and in that faithfulness take the difficult path of becoming a good friend to our own going.

Friendship transcends disappearance: an enduring friendship goes on after death, the exchange only transmuted by absence, the relationship advancing and maturing in a silent internal conversational way even after one half of the bond has passed on.

But no matter the medicinal virtues of being a true friend or sustaining a long close relationship with another, the ultimate touchstone of friendship is not improvement, neither of the self nor of the other; the ultimate touchstone is witness: the privilege of having been seen by someone and the equal privilege of being granted the sight of the essence of another, to have walked with them and to have believed in them, and sometimes just to have accompanied them for however brief a span, on a journey impossible to accomplish alone.

is unpreventable; the natural outcome of caring for people and things over which we have no control, of holding in our affections those who inevitably move beyond our line of sight. Even the longest, strongest marriage has had its heart broken many times just in the act of staying together.

Heartbreak begins the moment we are asked to let go but cannot: in other words, it colours and inhabits and magnifies each and every day; heartbreak is not a visitation, but a path that human beings follow through even the most average life. Heartbreak is an indication of our sincerity: in a love relationship, in a life's work, in trying to learn a musical instrument, in the attempt to shape a better more generous self. Heartbreak is the beautifully helpless side of love and affection and is just as much an essence and emblem of care as the spiritual athlete's quick but abstract ability to let go. Heartbreak has its own way of inhabiting time and its own beautiful and trying patience in coming and going.

Heartbreak is how we mature; yet we use the word heartbreak as if it only occurs when things have gone wrong: an unrequited love, a shattered dream, a child lost before their time. Heartbreak, we hope, is something we hope we can avoid; something to guard against, a chasm to be carefully looked for and then walked around; the hope is to find a way to place our feet where the elemental forces of life will keep us in the manner to which we want to be accustomed and which will keep us from the losses that all other human beings have experienced without exception since the beginning of conscious time. But heartbreak may be the very essence of being human, of being on the journey from here to there, and of coming to care deeply for what we find along the way.

If heartbreak is inevitable and inescapable, our only choice might be to look for it and make friends with it, to see it as our constant and instructive companion, and even perhaps, in the depth of its impact as well as in its hindsight, to see it as its own reward.

Heartbreak asks us not to look for an alternative path, because there is no alternative path. It is a deeper introduction to what we love and have loved, an inescapable and often beautiful question, something or someone who has been with us all along, asking us to be ready to let go of the way we are holding things and preparation perhaps, for the last letting go of all.

HEARTBREAK *We tend to think of 'enlightenment' as an abstract, as being a state above all suffering, but Buddha asked his followers in very intimate terms to follow heartbreak to its very end, to see it as part of any ultimate understanding, in effect to say the very last goodbye, to be completely present to 'everything ceasing', to everything we are constantly being asked to let go of, to the very origin of our pain, and thereby to let it flower into something else. My wife and I ran into this lovely family group for only a very brief train ride through the mountains of central Japan, but the chemistry and poignancy of the encounter and the tidal manner in which they suddenly had to leave, and the image they left in my camera, waving to us from an obscure country station platform, seemed to embody all the hellos and goodbyes I had ever made.*

Long before I fell in love with the man, I fell in love with the poet for the way his words create an opening for all of us to find our own way into a sense of ground and home in our bodies and experiences, while casting a larger horizon to move into our future all at once.

As I was struggling up the Inca Trail in the mountains of Peru one birthday, many years ago, memorizing 'Everything is Waiting for You' (and cursing the many stairs that were indeed my 'mentor of things to come'), I carried a hastily scrawled, handwritten copy on a torn notebook page. A book such as the one you are reading would have fit perfectly in my pilgrim rucksack, a companion to the journey in the way that one wants to have a treasured friend and companion along the road.

I chose these poems because they have guided me through many difficult years – some lines becoming mantras for more boldly inhabiting a desired way of being in the world, helping me as I read, 'let your vulnerabilities walking on the cracked sliding limestone be this time, not a weakness, but a faculty for understanding what's about to happen'.

The poems and essays collectively ask us to live fully into each epoch of our lives – into the daily shifts, the ever-turning seasonalities, and the broader cycles of gain and grief that are a part of our maturation, native to every phase of life and every person.

The poems are both for the times of day when we experience the world through its nuanced shadings and transitions, and also for the seasons when the colorations of the sky and earth turn more radically through darkness and light.

These poems are also offered within the context of an epoch when our human spirits and imaginations need all the support they can get. In this time of great light and great darkness, volatility and change, rapid technological, geopolitical, and economic shifts, as David Whyte says, 'Each of us will be asked to reach deeper, speak more bravely, live more from the fierce perspectives of the poetic imagination; to find the lines, in effect, already written inside us: poetry does not take surface political sides, it is always the conversation neither side is having, it is the breath in the voice about to discover itself only as it begins to speak, and it is that voice firmly anchored in a real and touchable body, standing on the ground of our real, inhabited world, speaking from a source that lives and thrives at that threshold between opposing sides we call a society'.[1]

GAYLE KAREN YOUNG WHYTE
Langley
August 2019

[1] From David's 'Letter from the House 2017', www.davidwhyte.com

Photo Credits